CAYMAN DIVER'S GUIDE

Shlomo & Roni Cohen

D0826162

CAYMAN DIVER'S GUIDE

Shlomo & Roni Cohen

SEAPEN BOOKS

SEAPEN
© Copyright 1991 Shlomo & Roni Cohen
Printed in Israel at the Chavatzelet Press, Herzlia.

1st Printing 1990
2nd Printing 1991

A BOOK NOOK EDITION
P.O.Box 1551 Grand Cayman B.W.I.   Fax: (809) 947 5053

To our son ORION

ISBN: 965-362-0053

The Cayman Island Diver's Guide

Compiled by	**Shlomo Cohen** **with Martin Sutton**
Illustrations, Maps and Design	**Shlomo Cohen**
Production Director	**Roni Cohen**
Editorial Director	**Louise Shabat-Bethlehem**
Project Coordinator	**Ruby Eviatar**
Graphic Production	**Mark Bleiweiss**
Editorial Assistant	**Amy Vowell**
Diving Team	**Ofer Bar Oz** **Doron Taragan** **Roni Cohen**

Photographed by	**Ruby Eviatar**	8-9, 45, 60B, 62L, 67, 69R, 76 122B, 134T, 136T, 141T, 146B, 150T, 153B, 154, 164T, 165, 166B.
	Martin Sutton	12B, 16, 17T, 24, 28, 65, 82, 84T, 140T, 143T, 147T, 167B.
	Chris McLaughlin	14-15, 98-99, 100, 114-115.
	Mike Kelly	12T, 36, 48, 72, 174.
	Shlomo Cohen	32-33, 37, 39, 40, 41, 42-43, 47, 55, 56, 59, 60T, 61, 63, 64, 69L, 70-71, 73, 74, 77, 80-81, 85, 87, 92, 97, 101, 104, 106, 110, 112, 113, 119, 121, 122T, 125, 127, 128-129, 136B, 137, 138, 140B, 141B, 142T, 143B, 144B, 146T, 147CL, 148, 151B, 152TR&B, 153T, 155, 156, 157, 159, 160, 161, 162T, 163, 166T, 167TL&R, 168-169 186-187.
	David Pilosof	17B, 20, 43BC.
	Darvin Ebanks	78.
	Charlene Burch	142B, 145B, 147CR, 152TL.
	Ofer Bar Oz	139T&B, 146C.
	Wayne Hasson	96.
	Kurt Amsler	144T, 145B, 149B, 150B, 151T 158, 159B 162B.
	Leslie McClain	84B, 135T&B, 164B.
	Beth Shelton	51, 53, 83, 130, 134B, 145T, 175.
Aerial Photographs	**Chris McLaughlin, Marit Sutton** **Shlomo Cohen.**	

WITH GRATITUDE
OR 34 GOOD REASONS TO READ THIS PAGE!

No man, they say, is an island... Certainly, we of **SEAPEN** are convinced of this. The production of the **Cayman Diver's Guide** would have been inconceivable without the dedication, professionalism and expertise of many islanders. We share this tribute to some very special Caymanians with you in the knowledge that, someday, when your paths cross, you will value your encounters with them as deeply as we have done.

The people of **Fisheye** provided much of the drive and inspiration behind this book. We owe a particular debt of gratitude to **Martin Sutton, Eddie 'Speedy' Uditis, Susan Abbott**, and the rest of the gang, **Mike A. Hydes, David C. Weaver**, and **Duane Engstrom**, for their time, unfailing patience and sound organizational abilities. We felt thoroughly at ease with the Fisheye crew, and thoroughly at home in their fine condominiums. Many thanks also to **Ron Kipp, Laurie Sutton** and **Christine R. Lexau** of **Bob Soto's Diving** for their friendly support and assistance.

Spanish Cove will always be synonymous for us with stunning beauty and luxurious accommodation matched only by the graciousness and cooperation of our hosts: manager **Layman Scott**, dive master **Scott Roe, Leslie McClain**, our skipper who never skipped a beat, **Beth Shelton, Bert Kramer, Dave McKenna** and **Reg Creighton**. Their combined and individual contributions were invaluable. We had the pleasure of spending time at **Surfside**, too. Thanks to **Bob Carter**, and his beautiful colleagues **Sue Steere** and **Kim Fabrizio**, for all their help. **Peter Farrell**, also of **Surfside**, will no doubt remember the **SEAPEN** dive team as mechanics with a gift for mysticism capable of overcoming engine failure with a few mantras. Uncooperative engines aside, we thoroughly enjoyed our excursions with him. **Dennis Denton** of **Research Submersibles Limited** shared an entirely different kind of journey with us, enthralling us with the sights of the depths. Still on the subject of transportation, thanks to **Gregory Merren** of **Parrot's Landing** for use of his underwater scooters.

Our thanks also to **Stuart Freeman** of **Eden Rock**, a man who knows his grotto, and **Bob Cohen** of **Cohen Associates**, for helping to get us airborne. **Barbara Levey** and **Ed Powers** of **Undersea Photo & Dive Supply** provided unflagging moral support. We much appreciated the goodwill of **Rod McDowall** of **Red Sail Sport**, too.

Chris and **Donna McLaughlin** of **Photo Tiara**, located in **Divi Tiara** on Cayman Brac, developed our films, boosted our confidence and made their considerable photographic talents available to us. A special word of thanks goes to **Chris** for his superb aerial photography. Still at Divi Tiara, we would like to express our gratitude to **David Feinberg** for all his support.

Graham Gaiger, skipper of 'Brac Fever', infected us with his enthusiasm and excitement - both highly contagious. So it was a good thing that **Dr. Trevor Goldberg**, the flying physician of North Carolina, was in the right place at the right time to help out. Seriously, Trevor's fine skills as a pilot were deeply appreciated. Our thanks are also due to **Mike Kelly** for his photographs, and to **Paul Schutt** of **Helix** Chicago, who has always been deeply supportive of our projects.

If there is anyone we have neglected to thank by name, it is because so many people were of invaluable assistance in the production of this book. So wherever you are, thank you.

And finally, to the **people of the Cayman Islands**, the finest and the best, **thank you!**

CONTENTS

WHY CAYMAN?

The man was exhausted, desperate, close to utter defeat. He had fallen prey to malaria, his ships were rotting and many of his crew had been massacred. He felt old beyond his years. There was no escaping his failure. The time had come to turn back. Christopher Columbus, "The Admiral of the Ocean Sea," on his fourth attempt to discover a route to Cathay (China) knew that this would be his last voyage. All the same, to his dying day, the dogged explorer believed that he had, indeed, reached China.

On the 16th of April 1503, overcome with fatigue, Columbus gave Diego Mendez command over his flagship, and ordered him to proceed from their position off Puerto Bello (present day Panama) to Hispaniola (The Dominican Republic). Columbus was sure that Hispaniola lay to the northeast. His men, weary of the hardships of their seemingly interminable voyage, argued that it lay directly to the north. The vanquished Columbus had by now lost the last vestiges of his authority. He gave in to the demands of the crew. Ironically, his calculations were correct — but the ships proceeded north. They made the Caribbean crossing in twenty-four days, and on the 10th of May 1503, land was sighted: the Cayman Islands. Ferdinand Columbus, the Admiral's son and biographer, made a log entry recording that: "We were in sight of two very small and low islands, full of tortoises (turtles), as was all the sea about, insomuch that they looked like little rocks for which reason these islands were called Tortugas."

Just as in Ferdinand's account, animals figure prominently in other early descriptions of the place. The so-called Turin map of 1523 names the Islands "Lagartos" which means "alligators" or "large lizards," a name supplanted in 1530 by the term "Caymanas" deriving from the Carib Indian word for the marine crocodile. Sir Francis Drake, who led an English expedition to the Caribbean in 1586, was familiar with this designation. He wrote: "There are on the island great serpents called Caymanas like large lizards," and confidently concluded his account with the information that they were edible! It seems that crocodiles once roamed in large numbers on Little Cayman, the island visited most frequently by early explorers. At any rate, the name stuck, but in the course of time, the crocodile population vanished from the spot!

So did Columbus! Three days after sighting the Caymans, he and his crew reached the southern shores of Cuba which he recognized from previous voyages. Hispaniola lay far out of reach, so the expedition limped its way across to Jamaica. Here they beached their ships and turned them into makeshift shelters. It was hardly a fitting climax to the last voyage of the great Columbus!

The Caymans, then, were to be the Admiral's final discovery. Like the signature of an artist concluding a masterpiece, Columbus signed his life's work with a flourish: the Cayman Islands.

Shlomo Cohen
Spanish Cove
July 1989

11

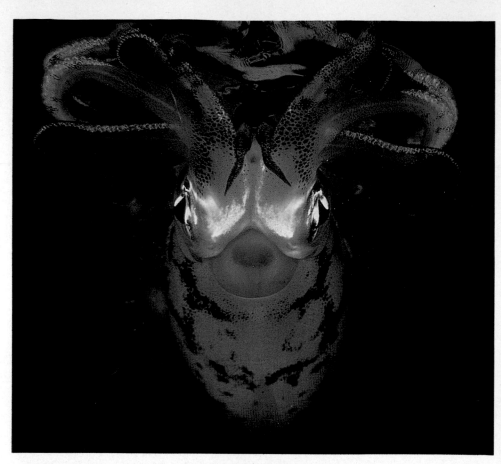

Two outstanding Squid portraits by Mike Kelly (top) and Martin Sutton (bottom)

INTRODUCTION

A FLOW OF HISTORY

The early history of the Cayman Islands must be seen against the background of seventeenth century superpower rivalry. Having discovered the "New World," the Spanish were in no hurry to share it! In fact, they denied the English the right to establish colonies or to conduct trade in the newly discovered territories of the Caribbean and South America. It was only after the defeat of the Spanish Armada that the English were able to establish a presence in the Caribbean. One of the first seafarers to do so was Captain William King, who, in his own words, "landed at Grand Caiman, being the westernmost, where we found no people, but a good river of fresh water; and there we turned up three score great tortoises" — two of which giants sufficed to feed ten men for a day. Over the next fifty years, the Caymans were increasingly used as a provisions stop by sailors anxious to avoid scurvy, or by bold buccaneers with a liking for turtle soup!

Ancient graves, erroneously said to be the graves of pirates

In 1654, Oliver Cromwell sought to expel the Spanish from the Caribbean, and recruited five regiments of soldiers for an expedition led by Admiral Sir William Penn and General Robert Venables. After suffering defeat at St. Domingo, this army successfully invaded Jamaica. Tradition has it that two of the first settlers in the Caymans were deserters from the army in Jamaica, named Bodden and Watler (a corruption of the name Walter, perhaps). They were joined by a handful of British settlers who were promised tax-free privileges and freedom from military service in return for colonizing the Caribbean. Some settlers subsequently brought "slaves and servants" to the Islands, whose slave population increased when, in 1781, an African slave ship was wrecked here and many slaves were sold to cover the costs of salvage. The last slave was sold in the Caymans almost a full century later, in October 1880.

But settled life on the farms and plantations was not all the Caymans offered. The entire Caribbean had long been host to privateers: English sailors operating under royal patronage who would plunder Spanish ships and settlements in order to gain access to the wealth and resources forbidden them by the Spanish kings. With the Treaty of Utrecht in 1713, privateers — whose activities were given official approval — were replaced by a series of legendary pirates, including the fearsome Edward Thatch or Teach, better known as Blackbeard, one of the many buccaneers who anchored off Hogstyes or Stake Bay! To this day, tales of hoards of Spanish pieces of eight continue to attract hopeful treasure hunters.

Grand Cayman — general overview

If the history of the Caymans abounds in romantic stories of privateers and pirate gold, it also includes incidents of outstanding bravery. One such story concerns the famous Wreck of the Ten Sail. One stormy November night back in 1788, the leading ship in a convoy of ten merchantmen collided with a reef in Gun Bay at the East End of Grand Cayman. Unfortunately, its warning signal to the other members of the convoy was tragically misinterpreted as an order to close ranks, and they, too, struck the reef. Undaunted by the turbulent seas, the East End villagers heroically rescued many lives. Legend has it that King George III of England was so impressed by their actions that he freed Caymanians from taxation in perpetuity! So the Wreck of the Ten Sail had far-reaching consequences, as the prolific number of banks operating in the Caymans today clearly attests! Hurricanes and devastation frequently disrupted life on the Islands. As recently as November 1932, almost every dwelling on Cayman Brac was destroyed by a particularly savage hurricane which ravaged the island for two days. Relief was slow in coming, one consequence of the isolation of the Caymans which only ended with the establishment of an airfield in Grand Cayman in 1953, to be followed by a second airstrip at Cayman Brac in 1954. Airline services meant tourists, and the Cayman Islands have never looked back. Today, this prosperous British dependency is the diving mecca of the Caribbean diving meccas, which brings us to the point of this book. From now onwards, let the flow of history flow underwater!

Caymanian Iguana

LOCATION

The Cayman Islands comprise a cluster of three islands centrally located in the northern Caribbean Sea. They are situated roughly in the middle of a circle formed by Cuba to the northeast, Jamaica to the east, the Honduras and Nicaragua to the southwest and Mexico, Belize and the Yucatan Peninsula to the west. By far the largest of the three, Grand Cayman (35km/22 miles in length, 6-12km/4-8 miles in width) lies some 776 km/485 miles south of Miami, Florida. With its 22,000 residents, representing an estimated 90% of the entire population of the Colony, Grand Cayman outshadows in its size and significance the two very much smaller sister islands of Cayman Brac and Little Cayman which lie some 128km/80 miles to the northeast. Cayman Brac is a narrow, elongated island (19km/12 miles in length and 3.2km/2 miles in width). Its population of 1,100 seems teeming in comparison with the 30 or so permanent residents of Little Cayman (16km/10 miles in length and 1.6km/1 mile in width). The spectacularly rich marinescape common to all three islands is the outcome of a shared set of geomorphological features.

GEOMORPHOLOGY

The Caribbean Sea is separated from the Mexican Gulf by an elongated trench which begins in the region of Haiti and Cuba and runs from east to west until it reaches the shores of Guatemala. This deep, elongated Cayman Trench actually forms part of a fault zone which originates east of Puerto Rico, passing to the north of Haiti and the Dominican Republic and south of Cuba, before bisecting Guatemala and eventually meeting up with the Middle American Trench. It was activity along this fault zone that led to the wholesale destruction of Guatemala City by earthquake back in 1974.

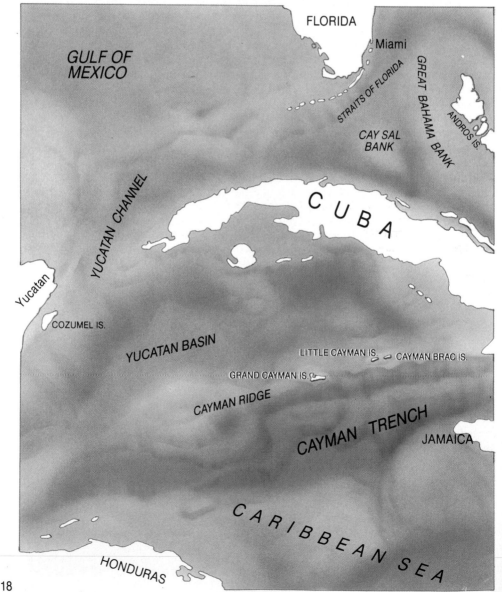

The northern edges of the Trench form the massive wall known as the Cayman Ridge. Three of its peaks break the water surface as three discrete towers to constitute the flat-topped Cayman Islands. The sheer size of the Cayman Ridge is impressive, to say the least. Its height (or depth) extends to some 8,400m/25,200ft, which makes it the deepest point in the entire Caribbean Sea.

North of the Cayman Ridge, the sea becomes progressively deeper once more, creating the Yucatan Basin. Thus, the three Cayman Islands are completely surrounded by a series of deep underwater walls on all sides. This unique confluence of geomorphological features is responsible for the existence of the famous Cayman walls and dropoffs. The walls, together with such factors as climate, sea temperature and underwater currents, form the basis of the Caymans' uniquely complex and multifaceted tapestry of underwater life.

WEATHER CONDITIONS

The Cayman Islands are blessed with fine weather all year round, thanks to the stabilizing influence of the surrounding Caribbean Sea, on the one hand, and thanks to their relative remoteness from continental North America, on the other, a factor which means that the Islands generally avoid being buffeted by winter storm fronts. It is also interesting to note that the Caymans' location relative to Jamaica often protects them from oncoming hurricanes which are deflected off the land mass of Jamaica and split in two, leaving the Caymans relatively unscathed.

Air temperatures during the summer months range between 80-90°F (about 30-40°C), and drop only slightly in winter to 70°F (roughly 20°C). Significantly for divers, water temperatures are constantly mild, with a winter low of about 77°F (25°C) and a summer high of 82°F (28°C). Even so, wetsuits or skeens are recommended, especially in view of the protection that they offer against corals.

Water visibility is generally excellent, except when stronger than usual currents prevail, and even then their influence is usually restricted and fairly local. Visibility in the North Wall region of Grand Cayman varies with high and low tide. Grand Cayman dive operators boast that they can guarantee diving 365 days a year. And it's perfectly true. Even if high seas and poor water visibility make diving impossible on one side of the island, you can always cross over to the other side and dive there!

AIRLINE SERVICES, CUSTOMS AND IMMIGRATION

The dawning of the jet age ended once and for all the traditional isolation and inaccessibility of the Cayman Islands. Flight time from Miami (lying 776 km/485 miles to the north) is a mere 1.5 hours, and from Houston (1952km/1,190 miles north) only 2.5 hours. Three major airlines run direct flights daily between the U.S. and the Islands: Cayman Airways, Northwest Airlines and Eastern Airlines (Eastern Airlines are inactive at the time of writing this book). Cayman Airways and Executive Air, a charter service, fly from Grand Cayman to both Cayman Brac and Little Cayman several times a week. You are reminded to reconfirm your return flight reservations no later than 72 hours before take-off.

Cayman immigration law requires proof of citizenship, a completed immigration entry form which will be supplied to you during the course of your flight, and a return air ticket. U.S. or Canadian citizens may present a voter's registration card or birth certificate instead of a passport, but a driver's license is not considered an acceptable form of identification. British and Commonwealth subjects (Canadians excepted) require a passport, but not a visa. Customs checks are thorough, and the Caymans have the most rigorous anti-drug laws in the entire Caribbean region. Violators, visitors included, found to possess drugs face immediate arrest, jail terms of up to ten years and fines of up to $20,000. Being a tourist is certainly not cause for exemption!

LOCAL CURRENCY

The official currency of the Cayman Islands is the C.I. dollar, which is worth U.S. $1.20 in terms of an International Monetary Fund agreement. Most restaurants and shops convert at a rate of C.I. $1.00 = U.S. $1.25 to cover bank charges. U.S. dollars are readily accepted, but more often than not you will receive C.I. dollars as change on your transaction. Credit cards are widely, but not universally, accepted so you are well advised to use travelers checks.

TRANSPORTATION

Unless you are staying at a resort on the comparatively remote East End or North Side of Grand Cayman, in which case your resort will provide a courtesy van, you will have to take a taxi to your hotel. Car rental is also an attractive alternative for the duration of your stay. On presenting a valid driver's license from your home state, you will be issued with a visitor's driving permit by the rental agency. One implication of the Cayman Islands' colonial affiliation is that one drives on the left side of the road!

TELEPHONE SERVICES, ELECTRICITY

Direct dialing is possible between the Caymans, the U.S., U.K. and Europe. When in the Caymans, five digit local numbers are used.

The Cayman Islands power system runs on 110 volt AC at 60 cycles, and is consequently fully compatible with that of the U.S. Electrical converters and outlet adapters are unnecessary, unless you hail from Europe.

SIGHTSEEING

Non-divers do not despair! The Caymans offer a host of sightseeing options which you can take in alone, or together with your diving companion after the day's dives. Sites of interest include:

Conch Shell House — a private home constructed out of thousands of conch shells.

The historic **Old Pink House** — a traditional Cayman residence over a century old but still occupied.

Hell — an aptly named limestone rock formation which looks as if it just emerged from a thorough roasting in the infernal ovens. A post office is located next to this strangely blackened rock pit. Any postcards you mail here will be postmarked 'Hell, Grand Cayman!' — an original supplement to your 'wish you were here' greeting.

Hell

The Cayman Turtle Farm — Historically turtles, not dive sites, were the Cayman Islands' biggest attraction. The turtle farm is home to more than 10,000 of these placid creatures and offers an engrossing tour covering their fascinating lifecycle, as well as the farming operation.

The Cayman Maritime and Treasure Museum — this George Town museum constructed by Herbert Humphreys, a renowned treasure hunter, gives visitors a firsthand look at sunken pirate treasure.

In addition, the **Atlantic Submarine Tours** company conducts tours from its sub *Atlantis,* certified to descend to a depth of 50m/150ft. One of the highlights offered is a visit to the wreck of the *Carrie Lee,* 40m/120ft down below. Floodlit night dives are particularly dramatic!

For more intrepid explorers, the **Research Submersibles Limited** company (RSL) specializes in unforgettable deep submersible trips 267m/800ft down along the face of Grand Cayman's spectacular dropoffs, stopping at the wreck of the *Kirk Pride* located at this tremendous depth. You will find this a truly compelling experience in a universe which exists way beyond the 43m/130ft safe Scuba limit! (See page 86).

UNDERSTANDING THE CAYMAN REEF FORMATION

As we have already noted, the Cayman Islands are a series of underwater mountain peaks surrounded by deep water. Consequently, their dive sites lie extremely close to the shore, sometimes even within swimming distance of it. The basic structure of the reef formation is fairly uniform and varies little from area to area. Its general features are schematically described below. Understanding the reef formation will enable you to find your way around more easily, thus enhancing your diving enjoyment.

CORAL HEADS
OR PATCH REEF

FRINGING REEF

In general, it is possible to divide the reef into three major areas. The first region slopes almost imperceptibly down from the shoreline. This **sandy expanse** is frequently covered with **turtle grass** and usually ends in a **fringing reef** made up of **elkhorn** or **staghorn corals** with small **coral heads.** The fringing reef marks the boundary of what is in essence a sort of placid lagoon.

The second area starts off as a moderately inclined **sand plain** covered in clusters of coral heads, otherwise termed **patch reef.** These progressively give rise to the **spur and groove system** which is so characteristic of the Caymans (see the explanation of terms below). In certain areas, the resultant formation is level and very wide (as is the case with **The Aquarium** or **Spanish Anchor,** pages 76 and 77). Elsewhere the coral heads are more pronounced and form a labyrinth of caves and canyons (like **Devil's Grotto,** on page 90 for instance), or even mini- walls (like **Spanish Bay Reef,** page 58).

After the sand plain, the reef descends steeply creating a third area which ends in the **dropoff** or **wall.** In some locations, the second and third reef areas merge into one another, and the coral heads form large **pinnacles** which are actually part of the ceiling of the wall.

PLAN YOUR DIVE AND DIVE YOUR PLAN

Diving in the Caymans generally takes place under the watchful eyes of experienced guides who have an unparalleled knowledge of the individual dive sites. So it is wise to rely on their dive plans. But regardless of whether you are diving in a group or independently (accompanied by your dive-partner, of course), establish your planned course, bottom time and safety stops before you begin diving.

A day of diving in the Caymans typically includes a deep first dive, followed by a short rest and then a shallow dive at the same spot, or at another suitably shallow site. In order to understand the descriptions of the dive sites in this book, or the instructions of the local Caymanian dive guides for that matter, familiarize yourself with the following terms used in connection with the reef formation:

A **pinnacle** is a frequently encountered feature consisting of a large block of coral which rears up in the shape of a tower. The pinnacle is more prominent than the surrounding **spur** to which it is usually connected, although you will sometimes come across large, isolated pinnacles like the one at **Ghost Mountain** (see page 56). Spurs are long strips or fingers of rock and coral separated by deep sandy channels, known as **canyons** or **grooves.** The spurs are sometimes so close to one another that they meet above the grooves, and take on the appearance of a **tunnel.** Tunnels are also termed **crevices, ravines** or **swim-throughs.** The term **chimney,** on the other hand, refers to a completely sealed horizontal cave (see **Bloody Bay Wall** on page 124), or a partly closed hollow canyon which begins at the **wall lip,** or edge, and continues halfway down the length of the wall, extending to the sea floor at times. The wall lip lies at an average of 15-20m (45-60ft), and dives are planned up to a depth of 33m (100ft). The **wall** or **dropoff** is actually the end of the **shelf,** the point at which the really deep water begins. Sometimes it takes the form of a very steep sand slope, while elsewhere it is a steep wall fissured by caves and canyons where protruding pinnacles are very much in evidence. In certain locations, the wall is obliterated behind a veritable waterfall of sand, originating in the sand plain above it. This spectacular river of sand is called a **sand chute.** Whatever their specific make-up, walls and dropoffs are what diving in the Caymans is all about.

Most dives are similar in general outline. Set off from the **mooring,** which is generally located some 10-15m (30-45ft) above the sand plain. Continue through the grooves and canyons to

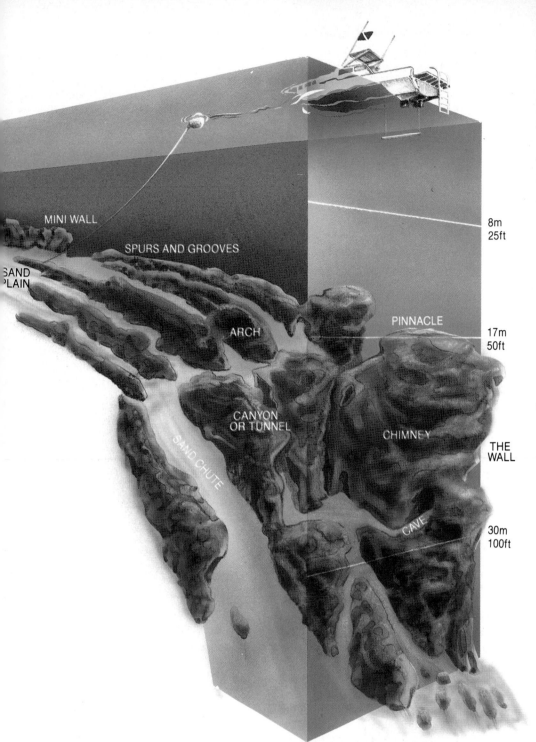

MINI WALL

SPURS AND GROOVES

SAND PLAIN

ARCH

PINNACLE

CANYON OR TUNNEL

SAND CHUTE

CHIMNEY

THE WALL

CAVE

8m 25ft

17m 50ft

30m 100ft

the wall (even if your boat is located above the wall itself, depending on such factors as wind and current). Your guide will take you through a different groove on your way back to the mooring rope, which you ascend to perform a safety stop. Most dive boats are equipped with a **safety bar** which is lowered into the water to a depth of 3m (10ft) to let you rest comfortably during the safety stop. A regulator and extra tank are usually suspended below the boat, too. If there is a strong current, a float will be lowered for you to grasp should the current carry you off. Since your guide is intimately familiar with wind and water conditions, don't hesitate to ask questions before setting off on your dive.

Remember one important principle: most spur and groove systems point in the general direction of the shore. They resemble fingers stretching from dry land out to sea, that is from shallow to deep water and the dropoff. Should you lose your group in the vicinity of the wall, **do not** ascend to the surface to decide on the direction home. Simply enter a groove and swim along it. In most cases, it will lead you to shallow water where you should be able to locate the mooring rope.

AVOIDING DIVER DAMAGE

The coral reefs of the Caymans are home to over a thousand organisms which interact in a complex, yet fragile, equilibrium. The very reef itself is animate — corals, gorgonian corals (sea-fans, sea whips, sea plumes) and sponges are animals not species of marine flora. These animals are in ongoing competition with marine algae, both striving to dominate their environment. And marine algae, the world's fastest growing life form, has a clear advantage over the slow coral whose growth rate ranges between 1.3-10cm (0.5-4in) per year. Remember that the huge, impressive coral heads of the Caymans were centuries in the making and that the slightest careless movement on your part can have immensely damaging consequences. In most stony corals, the living tissue is to be found in a thin layer on, or just below, the outer surface. So even a casual scrape from your tank or fins wounds the coral. Once damaged, the coral tries to grow back but may not be able to compete with the invasion of algae. Scarred, algae-covered coral is not particularly attractive. But more significantly, the entire reef equilibrium is affected by damage to live coral. Even a seemingly slight reduction in live coral cover will have an adverse chain effect on the kinds of fish species found, on their numbers, as well as on marine invertebrates.

So keep the following tips in mind to reduce diver damage:
Be as graceful, fluid and controlled in your movements as possible. Restrict unnecessary hand movements to a minimum. Stay horizontal while finning well above the coral or sea floor. Avoid stirring up murky clouds of sediment or sand, not only to ensure good visibility and clear underwater photographs, but also because corals and sponges have a very low tolerance for sediment. Overweighting, a common mistake of novice divers, will tend to make you clumsy and accident prone, while wearing gloves may render you insensitive to the incredible fragility of the reef. Never grab at, or kneel on, coral. Be aware of the location of your console and octopus. Don't drag them insensitively behind you, allowing them to snag on the coral and to leave a trail of destruction in your wake. Enjoy the reef animals from afar. Inconsiderate behavior like trying to climb into barrel sponges, turning over rocks, attempting to handle porcupine fish and so on will threaten a particular life form or destroy its habitat. The illegal cutting up of long-spined black urchins for fish food nearly brought about their extinction in these waters. Leave the urchins alone — they help keep the algae in check.

Finally, in terms of the Cayman Marine Conservation Laws, it is a serious criminal offence to:
- take any marine life anywhere while on Scuba
- take any corals, sponges, etc. from any Cayman waters
- possess a spear gun without a license from the Cayman Marine Conservation Board
- export fish or any other marine life
- take or molest a turtle

Law enforcement is strict, and offenders face heavy penalties.

Dive 'The Manta' for real Wall-to-Wall Adventure.

A FAST 25 KNOT CRUISE TO EAST & NORTH WALLS

GRAND CAYMAN

Sunset House

CARIBBEAN SEA

N

Photo: Cathy Church

There's a whole new reason to dive Grand Cayman again.

Miles of untouched reefs and drop-offs on the Island's North and East coasts are now accessible to Sunset House divers.

'The Manta' is the latest addition to Sunset House's fleet of dive boats. Our sleek 45 foot power catamaran whisks small groups of experienced divers to isolated sites on all-day, 3-tank expeditions.

For the first time, serious divers get all of the excitement of Cayman's remote, wild areas. Plus the many creature comforts of Sunset House.

So we're welcoming back friends who have always loved the warmth of this family-run Hotel. Divers who enjoy the Hotel for divers by divers. The Manta is just one of the many benefits that we offer at Sunset House.

We're also the home of the world-famous Cathy Church School of Underwater Photography. Here you'll find all that you need to capture the adventure of your dive vacation on film.

So if the idea of the ultimate dive excites you why not find out more? For more details or to make your reservation call Sunset House direct at 809-949 7111 or toll-free from the US on 1-800 854 4767.

CIWA

SUNSET HOUSE
Grand Cayman's Hotel For Divers By Divers

SUMMARY OF CAYMAN ISLANDS MARINE CONSERVATION LAWS

PROTECTION OF CERTAIN SPECIES

1. **Lobsters:**
   - Only spiny lobsters may be taken.
   - Minimum size: 3½ inches cape length or 6 inches tail length.
   - Limit: five lobster per person per day or fifteen per boat per day, whichever is less.
   - Closed season: February 1 through July 31.

2. **Conch:**
   - Catch limit: 15 per person per day or 20 per boat per day.
   - No one may purchase or receive more than 20 conch per day from Cayman waters.

3. **Turtles:**
   - Possession of turtle eggs prohibited except for those so licensed.
   - May take turtles only with licence - licences given only to those who have traditionally taken turtles in Cayman waters, subject to the following conditions:
     - Closed season: May 1 through October 31.
     - Limit: six per licensed fisherman per season.
     - No use of spearguns or harpoons.
     - Minimum size: 120 pounds for green turtles; 80 pounds for hawksbill and loggerhead.
     - Must be tagged and approved by fisheries officer before slaughter.

4. **Groupers:**
   - Three restricted areas designated for protection of spawning groupers: Coxswain Bank off East End, Grand Cayman; Grouper Hole northeast of Little Cayman; and an area off the northeast point of Cayman Brac.
   - Only people normally resident in the Cayman Islands may enter these areas.
   - Within these areas, fishing by spear gun, fish trap and any kind of net is prohibited. Line fishing only permitted.

5. **Other species:**
   - No taking any coral, algae, sponges or turtle eggs.
   - No taking hermit crabs except in reasonable quantities for fish bait or human consumption.

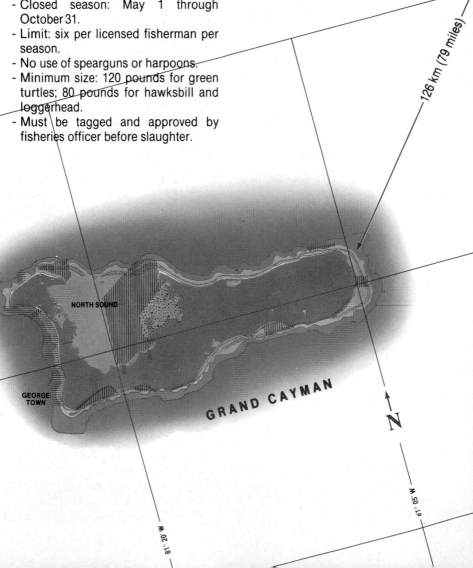

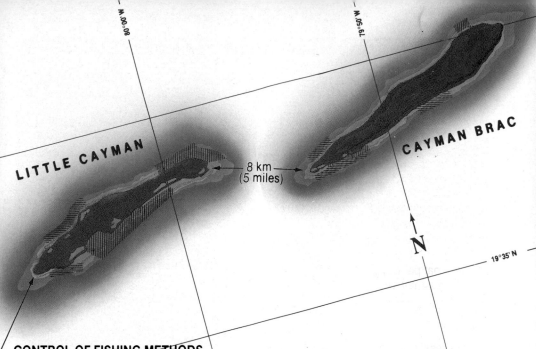

LITTLE CAYMAN

CAYMAN BRAC

←— 8 km —→
(5 miles)

N

19°35' N

CONTROL OF FISHING METHODS

1. **No taking of ANY kind of marine life while on scuba**

2. Fishing with poison or noxious substance prohibited.

3. **Spear Guns:**
   - No one may use a spear gun in Cayman unless licensed by the Marine Conservation Board.
   - Spear guns may not be used in any Marine Park area: Replenishment Zone, Marine Park Zone or Environmental Zone.
   - Catch limit: six fish per day, of which no more than three may be of the same species.
   - Importation of spear guns and parts prohibited.

4. **Gill nets prohibited**

5. **Seine nets:**
   - Each net must be licensed by the Marine Conservation Board.
   - Cannot be used on Little Cayman or in any Replenishment, Marine Park or Environmental Zone.

GENERAL RULES

1. Export of live fish or other marine life prohibited.

2. No effluent or raw sewage may be dumped into Cayman waters.

3. No cutting, carving, mutilating, moving, displacing or breaking any underwater coral, plant growth or formation without a licence from the Governor.

ENFORCEMENT

Violation of these laws is an offence carrying a maximum penalty of a $5000 fine and one year in jail. Upon conviction, forfeiture of the trap, net, diving equipment and/or vessel may also be ordered.

RULES FOR CAYMAN ISLANDS MARINE PARKS

REPLENISHMENT ZONE
- No taking conch or lobster by any means.
- Line fishing and anchoring are permitted.
- Spear guns, pole spears, fish traps and nets prohibited, except that fry and sprat may be taken with a fry or cast net.

ENVIRONMENTAL ZONE
- No taking of any marine life, alive or dead, with no exceptions.
- No anchoring of any boat.
- No in-water activities.

[NOTE: Line fishing, fish traps, seine nets, spear guns and pole spears totally prohibited.]

MARINE PARK ZONE
- No taking any marine life alive or dead, except:
  - Line fishing from shore is permitted.
  - Line fishing at and beyond the dropoff is permitted.
  - Taking fry and sprat with a fry or cast net is permitted.

[NOTE: Fish traps, spear guns, pole spears, seine nets totally prohibited.]

- No anchoring - use of fixed moorings only, except:
  - Boats of sixty feet or less may anchor in sand, so long as no grappling hooks are used, and neither the anchor nor the rope or chain lies on coral.
  - Anchoring permitted in designated Port anchorage areas.
  - Anchoring prohibitions suspended during emergencies and by permission of Port Director.

27

Rum Point 24.5 m.
East End 19 m.
North Side 19 m.
West Bay 6.5.
7-Mile Beach 3.5 m.
George Town 1.5 m.
Rodden Town 8.5 m.
avannah 5.5 m.

Cayman, the "little-big" island

Smith Cove, one of the island's many small coves

The smart choice!

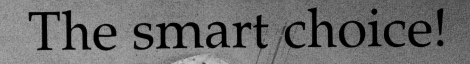

Make Morris your choice for underwater accessories. All Morris products are economically priced and built for years of reliable service. Our flash equipment, from the high-powered, self-contained F5-TTL (shown here) to the economical F3-TTL and our newest creation, the compact and cordless UW Slave Flash, is designed to make great pictures effortlessly. Our extension tube system for the Nikonos is the most versatile available. With our 3 tubes and 7 framers, you can shoot at 10 magnification ratios on land and underwater! We have 2 powerful flashlights and 2 signal strobes for the maximum in visibility and safety.

For more product information, contact your local dive shop, photo store or The Morris Co.

The Morris Co.
1205 West Jackson Blvd.
Chicago, Illinois 60607
312.421.5739

ABOUT THIS BOOK

The sea is a demanding mistress, the artist's muse no less so. So it is no wonder that I found the idea of creating a new diver's guide on the Cayman Islands so compulsive. Take an author-artist addicted to diving, add a spectacular dive location, throw in a camera and a few rolls of film, and you have a supremely powerful catalyst — as I had already proved with my previous books, the **Red Sea Diver's Guide** and the **Bahamas Diver's Guide.**

But the making of the **Cayman Diver's Guide** was to be a whole different kettle of fish. Unlike the other regions featured in our guides, divers seldom dive here without the assistance of resident dive operators. Nevertheless, the sheer complexity of the Caymans' marine topography often leaves divers with a blurred, hazy picture of what has been, or will be, encountered. True, SEAPEN's diving media revolution, based on a combination of incisive text and superb aerial photographs, constituted an excellent starting point. But I was looking for that elusive extra dimension which would make this book more than just another illustrated underwater guide.

It took repeated dives in the Caymans and the invaluable input of the local Caymanian operators to generate a solution. The answer came in the form of an integrated graphic-photographic presentation. Our composite three-dimensional format makes both for maximum ease in mentally mapping out a site as well as for stunning visual impact. In one glance, you can locate yourself simultaneously under the water and in relation to prominent on-shore landmarks. So the **Cayman Diver's Guide** relieves you of the burden of mere navigation, allowing you to deliver yourself wholly to the captivations of the Cayman marinescape.

Of course, this book does not presume to depict every dive site in the Caymans, a task way beyond the scope of a single volume. Rather, a representative number of sites have been selected according to two criteria: the beauty of a particular site on the one hand, and its popularity, on the other, judged in terms of its accessibility and whether it appears on the itineraries of local dive operators.

The sites chosen form a geographical continuum. The chapter on **Grand Cayman** covers its western section, that is the North Wall from Rum Point through to West Bay, and finally south to George Town. The chapter on **Cayman Brac** features its northwestern side, while that on **Little Cayman** portrays sites in the Bloody Bay area.

Sites are divided into two categories. Major sites comprise deep dives or dives of special interest, while secondary sites are usually shallow dives which might feature as your second dive on a particular dive agenda. In view of their considerable complexity, major sites are accompanied by detailed illustrations. Secondary sites receive a purely verbal description, given that dives are conducted relatively freely and independently in these shallow and topographically uncomplicated areas. Their importance should not, however, be underestimated. The combination of shallow water, good visibility and diving ease they offer encourages closer encounters with the reef population, and provides perfect opportunities for underwater photography.

The explanatory text has two parts. A general introductory section amplifying a site's calling card is situated top right. More specific descriptions relating to the dive itself, its route or points of special interest accompany the diagram to provide a complete portrait of each site.

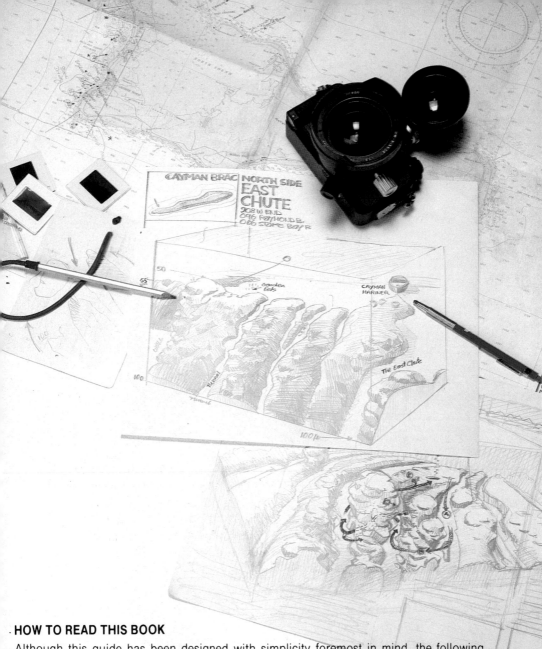

HOW TO READ THIS BOOK

Although this guide has been designed with simplicity foremost in mind, the following points will assist you in making it just that little bit more user-friendly.

The layout of the dive sites is consistent throughout the book, with slight variations in the perspective of the panoramas presented alone. At the top left hand corner of the page, you will find the calling card of each site, which includes its name, bearings (whether formal bearings or simply indications of well-known points of reference) and a schematic map displaying prominent landmarks, with a white arrow indicating your present location. (More detailed maps are to be found in the introductory sections of each chapter). The bearings are also repeated on the diagram of the site itself, together with arrows indicating the actual direction of the various landmarks. Given the characteristic perspective of these drawings, compass points may appear a little distorted at times.

The diagrams accompanying the text show the surface and the underwater marinescape simultaneously. Where necessary, diving routes are indicated using white arrows combined with alphabetical characters. Characters in circular frames are referred to in the body of the text. Characters in square frames refer to the photographs accompanying a given text, with arrows indicating the direction of the shot. General depth indications also appear on each diagram.

I am certain that the confidence that comes from glancing over a particular site description in this book before you actually dive will make your dive safer and more enjoyable, even if this is the very first time you are wetting your fins in the crystal waters of the Cayman Islands. 31

THE DIVING SITES
GRAND CAYMAN

GRAND CAYMAN

The Grand Cayman coastline is dotted with a multitude of diving sites whose fascination is apparent whenever and wherever you enter the water. Obviously, to describe each one of them in detail would be beyond the scope of this book. Therefore we have limited the sites treated to two major areas — the North Coast and the West Coast. In the map below, diving sites are classified as follows:

- ■ Detailed site description with diagram (page reference indicated)
- ★ General site description without diagram (page reference indicated)
- ● Well-known sites not treated in this book

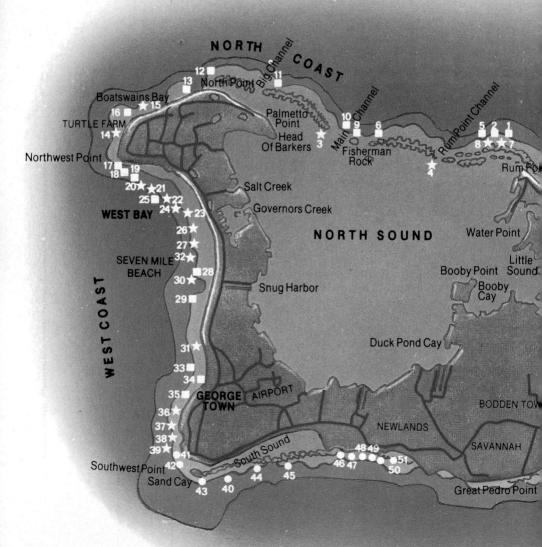

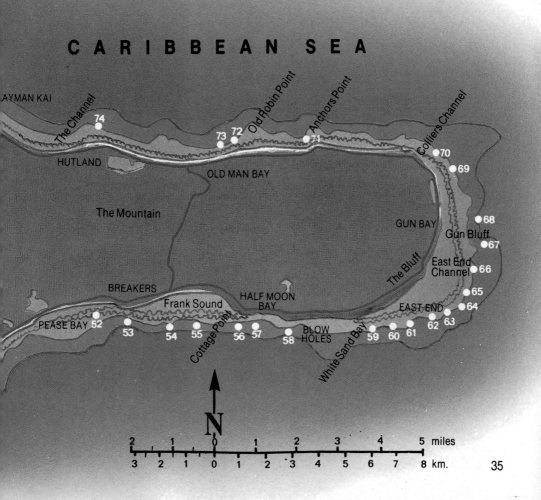

THE NORTH COAST

Two highly distinctive geographical features underlie the mystique of Grand Cayman's North Coast in diving circles. The first is, of course, the Great Cayman Wall, or North Wall, justly renowned for the sheer drama of its plummeting cliffs. Although it runs along the entire length of the North Coast from Collier Point in the east to Boatswains Point some 32km (20 miles) to the west, we have chosen to focus in this section on the 13km (9 mile) stretch between Rum Point and Boatswains Point. The Northwest Bay is usually a zone in itself, but we have included it in our definition of the North Coast.

The second attraction, less spectacular but equally rewarding, is the North Sound, a vast shallow lagoon extending in an irregular arc between Rum Point and Conch Point. Its bottom is sandy, and is covered with turtle grass, interspersed here and there with an occasional coral head. A fringing reef surrounds the entire lagoon, restricting access to three channels: Rum Point Channel in the east, the Main Channel in the center of the lagoon, and Boat Channel in the west. Almost all the beaches along the protected inner rim of the lagoon are densely overgrown with mangroves which flourish in these shallow, calm waters. The roots of these plants form a tangled submarine jungle — a natural breeding ground for a host of fish species.

This wealth of marine life along the inner sand flats of the Sound holds the key to its fascination. Molluscs, including trumpet triton, Caribbean conch, sunbursts, helmet shells and many others, inhabit the sandy floor of the lagoon and tilefish use shell fragments or coral chips to construct their tunnel abodes. Hermit crabs are less enthusiastic builders, and simply take over abandoned conch shells. Shy, diminutive sailfin blennies dart out at lightning speed in pursuit of prey, only to return within seconds to the security of their holes. So photographing a sailfin requires skill, perseverance and, above all, patience, in more than the usual proportions. The portrait of this intriguing creature which appears below is a fine tribute to photographer Mike Kelly's mastery of his craft.

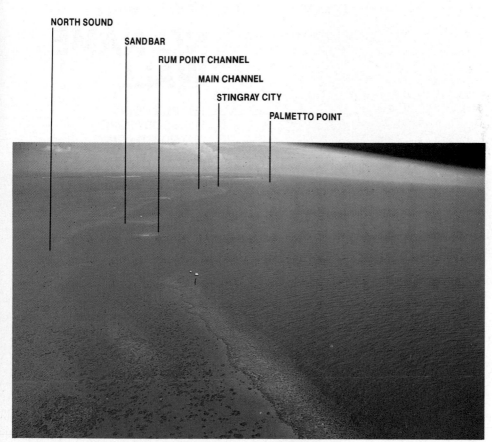

NORTH SOUND

SANDBAR

RUM POINT CHANNEL

MAIN CHANNEL

STINGRAY CITY

PALMETTO POINT

The North Coast fringing reef and channels as seen from Rum Point

Virtually any stretch of reef along the Great Cayman Wall, whose lip lies at an average depth of 13-20m (40-60ft), provides exceptional diving. Additionally, the proximity of sand plain, wall and open water leads to interesting encounters between open sea species (eagle rays, jacks and turtles), which penetrate the lagoon through openings in the reef, and more classical reef inhabitants.

Despite the variety of diving options along the North Coast, it tends to be less popular than the West Bay area for two reasons. Firstly, it is more susceptible to poor weather conditions. Strong north winds make for choppy seas and poor underwater visibility. Visibility is also affected by fluctuations in tide. Secondly, most dedicated dive resorts are located in the West Bay. Reaching the North Coast means a boat trip across the Sound or around the Cape, which wastes precious diving time.

Dive operators like Spanish Cove, situated slightly west of Conch Point, or Surfside, at Rum Point, will naturally take advantage of their respective locations to dive the North Coast more intensively.

Unlike the West Bay where diving sites are demarcated by buoys, this system is less rigidly adhered to along the North Coast. Although some sites are formally marked, others come into being the moment one of the skippers operating here decides to cast anchor. Each skipper has favorite diving sites and favorite names for these sites, so any given location may bear several names.

To summarize, the North Coast is important for its fascinating shallow dive sites, including the famous Stingray City, as well as for its excellent wall dives. Scarcely a dive goes by in deeper waters without the sighting of eagle rays, turtles, barracudas, jacks or an occasional shark — an integral part of your North Wall experience. So, weather permitting, don't overlook the opportunity to dive this stretch of coastline.

Over and above the general attractions already described, the North Coast is famed for three distinct diving sites: Stingray City, Sandbar and Tarpon Alley.

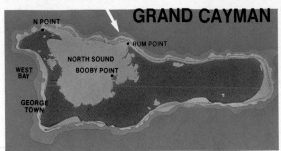

RUM POINT

FRINGING REEF

Once in the water, look for the first large pinnacle on the northernmost side. To the left of this pinnacle is a canyon which leads to a knee-like protrusion jutting out from the base of the pinnacle. You are now at a depth of about 25m (75ft) Ⓐ. Swim across the knee until you come to the first canyon which opens onto a wide cave Ⓑ. The cave narrows to meet the entrance of the adjacent canyon, and both lead up to to the sand plain. Continue swimming and magically the second pinnacle will appear. Hidden behind this pinnacle are two canyons well worth exploring. The third pinnacle in the series is characterized by its greater height with a base which is vertical and sheer Ⓒ. The upper part of this pinnacle is cut by a canyon-like structure which lies parallel to the wall. The base of this canyon opens up into a huge cave which leads to the wall lip.

If you plan to photograph, save your film for two areas in particular: the third pinnacle which is covered by black corals and many colorful sponges growing from the wall, and the fascinating grooves and spurs in the sand plain area.

No Name Wall is the easternmost site in the North Wall series. This diving ground is especially exhilarating because of its many canyons, tunnels and caves, and because the wall is sheer and vertical in several places. The upper part of the wall is a sand plain covered with coral heads. It is furrowed by a system of spurs and grooves that begin at the fringing reef and extend out to the wall. Three pinnacles and four canyons or tunnels form No Name Wall. The wall starts at 18m (55ft) and drops to a depth of 30m (90-100ft.) The groove and spur formation above the wall is very beautiful with sandy paths that shimmer whitely as they curve in and out of the spurs.

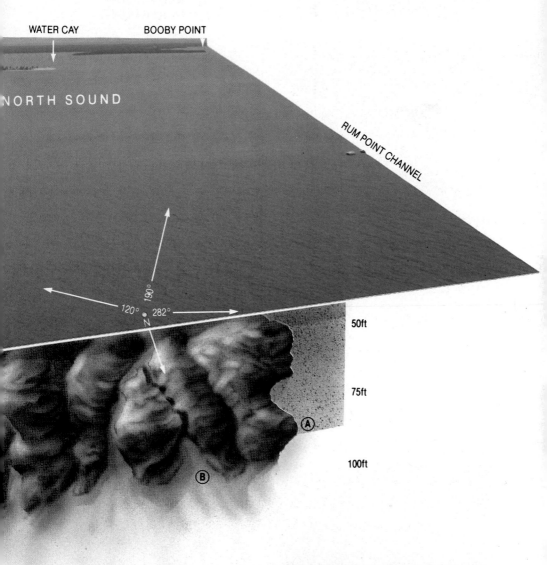

Tiger grouper in cleaning station on the wall lip.

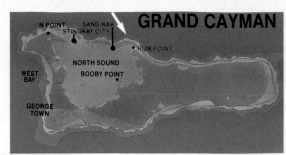

NORTH WALL
GALE'S MOUNTAIN

105° RUM POINT
185° BOOBY POINT
278° NORTH POINT

← RUM POINT

N O R T

FRINGING REEF

60ft

80ft

Sue Steere inside the canyon at Gale's Mountain Peak

Gale's Mountain is one of the most alluring sites in this area and should not be missed. The visual configuration of scattered spurs, grooves and canyons is unusually formed as if some angry sea god had once stamped his feet in rage and caused this deep-sea disturbance of structure and order. We don't think that you'll mind, however, as it makes for a fascinating dive. The site is located west of No Name Wall and almost opposite the entrance to Rum Point Channel. Although this site plunges down to 50m (150ft), the dive described here is not as deep as other dives since it focuses on the mountain peak which lies at a depth of 20m (60ft).

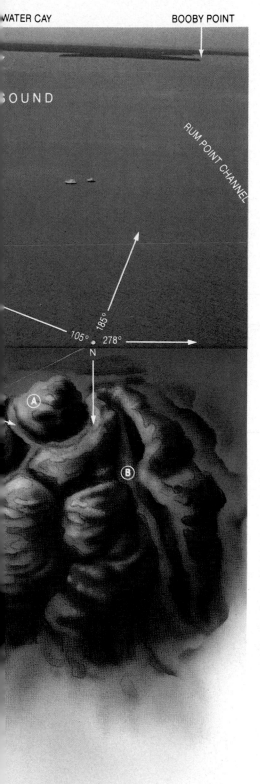

WATER CAY   BOOBY POINT

SOUND

RUM POINT CHANNEL

185°
105°   278°
N

(A)

(B)

Your first impression of Gale's Mountain will probably be of a huge pyramid of coral heads. The peak of this structure, width 15m (45ft), is a dome-like coral head separated from the rest of the mountain by curved tunnels at its conical base Ⓐ, width 60m (180ft).

The mooring line is situated on the sand plain behind the peak, so approach this site by diving north of the mountain peak and entering the sheer vertical canyon Ⓑ. A deep and winding ravine surrounds the mountain base and travels back up through a huge tunnel on the other side of the mountain Ⓒ No matter how enthralled you may be by the magnificence of this underwater mountain, do not disappoint the many eagle rays, schools of horse-eyed jacks and the occasional shark that may swim by hoping to impress you. The variety of colorful corals and sponges are easily photographed thanks to ideal light conditions at this shallow depth. The photographic subject matter here is captivating: the base of the dome with its seemingly isolated peak ᴅ appears illuminated and contrasts strongly with the surrounding tunnels and caves.

STINGRAY CITY AND SANDBAR

Visiting the Caymans without diving Stingray City is like not visiting the Caymans at all! The rays here are so tame that they have become one of the chief attractions of the entire Caribbean. In fact, tame rays are to be found both at Stingray City and at a newer site known as Sandbar.

The original Stingray City is located on the west side of the Main Channel, close to Barkers Cay. The site comprises a wide sandy channel covered with coral heads. Unfortunately, tidal variations sometimes have an adverse affect on underwater visibility here. Incidentally, while at Stingray City, look up another of its famous inhabitants — a green moray eel who is also exceptionally used to divers.

Sandbar lies at the entrance to Rum Point Channel. The water is very shallow at this point, and the sea floor is flat and sandy. In some places, you will find yourself standing in chest-high water.

Photographic conditions are absolutely ideal. Shafts of sun penetrate the crystal-clear water to scatter on the sandy bottom or on the stingrays themselves. But even perfection has its drawbacks. The main one here is precisely the popularity of the site. You will almost certainly have to vie for a prime position with many other aspirant photographers like yourself.

A word of caution about the rays: although tame, they are aggressive. That is to say, they will nudge or shove divers in the hope of being fed. The boisterousness of the rays can be highly alarming, but no actual attacks on divers have ever been recorded. Still, if you are unfamiliar with rays, or if this is your first dive in the area, don't rush into the water. Leap before you look, and you will be besieged by rays in a matter of seconds! Avoid having to waste precious time trying to evade the very creatures you came to meet by letting the more experienced divers go ahead of you. Once you observe that a pack of rays has congregated, enter the water cautiously at some distance from the group and concentrate on getting some spectacular shots. The photographs on these pages depict typical street scenes along the main boulevards of Stingray City and Sandbar!

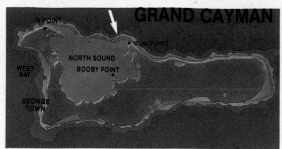

WATER CAY

RUM POINT

REEF

60ft

80ft

100ft

© (C)

The first canyon lies north of the 20m (60ft) deep sand plain. You will see the coral heads before you reach it as they rest in slightly shallower water, at about 17m (50ft). Enter the canyon Ⓐ through a cave-like opening and let it lead you down to 23m (70ft). You will find yourself in a clearing which meets up with another canyon. This passes out onto a small sand chute, another of the attractions of this scenic area. Turn east (right) and swim parallel to the wall until you discover three other canyons. Continue along this route and you will reach the highest pinnacle in this site. A prominent rhino horn of Bouder coral Ⓑ juts out from the pinnacle at about 27m (80ft). Behind this spectacular pinnacle is a white sandy canyon. Continue to swim east until you reach the third pinnacle which is characterized by a deep crack in its middle and a huge knee-like formation. Where the knee has separated from the pinnacle at 28m (85ft) a cave-like hollow can be seen Ⓒ. It is worth investigating this cave to experience the sudden drop. Circle around the knee in order to arrive at the entrance of the cave once more. Look out for a narrow elongated canyon before the knee. If you follow this canyon, it will lead you westward up to the sand plain where you can reach the mooring line.

Chinese Wall is located almost in front of the east side of Rum Channel. The vast size of this site poses an immense challenge that only careful planning can counter: if you intend to cover all of this area in the best possible time, plan your dive to run along the wall. At low tide, the fringing reef is easily visible. The sand plain is very wide and is characterized by fewer coral heads than the other diving sites. The relative scarcity of coral heads leaves the water jade green,which renders the site easily identifiable by boat. The steeply slanting wall explodes into a profusion of canyons. If you have the time, it is a thrilling experience to cover the whole length of two canyons in particular.

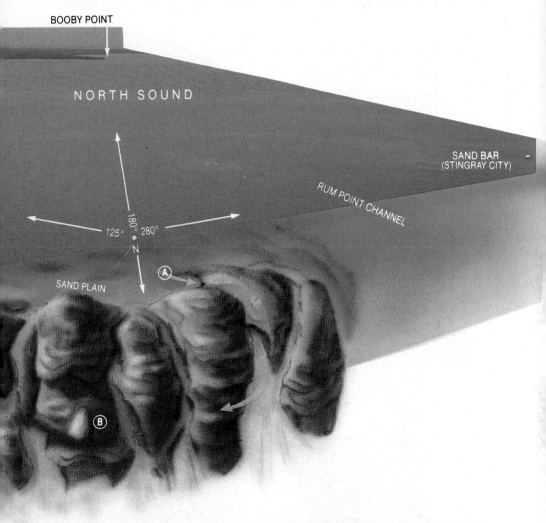

Honeycomb cowfish and orange tube sponge on the wall lip

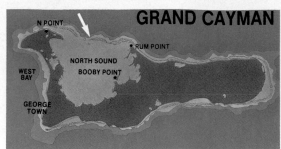

GRAND CAYMAN
NORTH WALL
LEMON DROPOFF

115° RUM POINT
280° NORTH POINT
220° EDGE OF THE FRINGING REEF

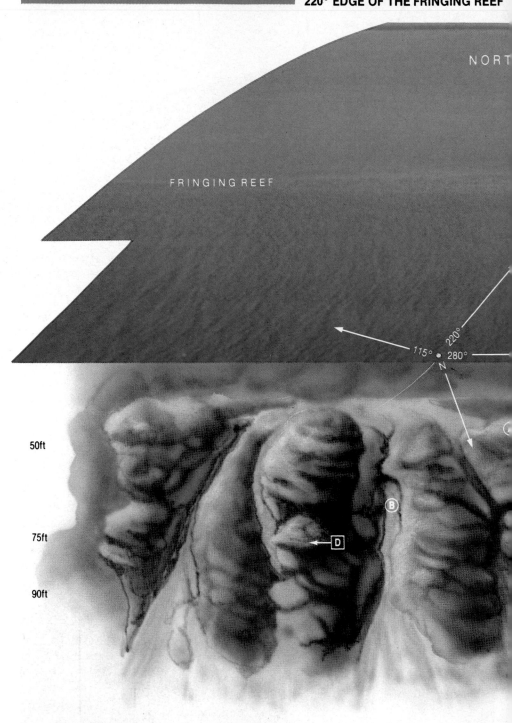

NORT

FRINGING REEF

115° 220° 280°

N

50ft

75ft

90ft

B

D

Lemon Dropoff is located directly opposite the edge of the fringing reef on the east side of the Main Channel. The site is characterized by three large pinnacles, each separated by an intricate system of canyons and sand chutes. It is rich in coral and open water fish, sponges, black corals and gorgonians. Lemon Dropoff was named after the lemon sharks which are said to frequent this area from time to time.

RAND CAYMAN

SOUND

STINGRAY CITY →

MAIN CHANNEL

The first pinnacle exudes a strong sense of the unexpected. Its upper part is rounded and its lower part plummets vertically to the sandy bottom Ⓐ.Two canyons lie to the east of this, the second one narrowing as it extends upwards to a coral cluster which forms a beautiful arching structureⒷA huge step cuts into the middle of the second pinnacle. Sponges and corals grow abundantly in this area, making it an outstanding spot for wide angle and macro shots. The highest of the trio is the third pinnacle with a jutting-out step and a long sandy canyon which leads up to the sand plain. Enjoy the peace and tranquility of this relatively unexplored deep diving site.

Ⓓ

GRAND CANYON

The entire region of the North Wall opposite Rum Point Channel is extremely rich in large coral heads and canyons which offer plentiful diving opportunities. One site worthy of special attention is the Grand Canyon which lies to the west of **Gale's Mountain**. It is hard to exaggerate the immensity of this horseshoe canyon, bounded by massive coral buttresses 50m (150ft) apart. It is important not to get carried away by the dramatic scenery of the Grand Canyon, which might tempt you to exceed safe depth limits.

THE PINNACLES

Along much of the North Wall, the area between the dropoff and the fringing reef abounds in shallow dive sites well suited to conducting your second dive. One such site, The Pinnacles, lies 180m (200 yards) south of **Gale's Mountain**. Here, the sand plain is furrowed by long spurs some of which culminate in small pinnacles. This spot is ideal for macro photography of such enticing subjects as arrow crabs, tube worms, spotted drums and cleaning gobies with their clients.

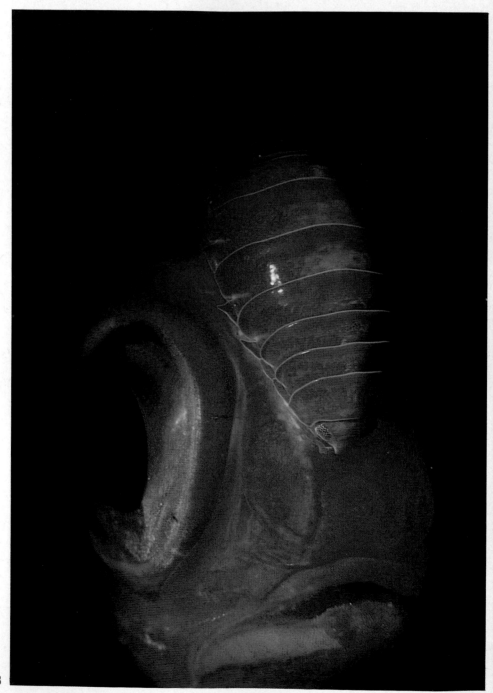

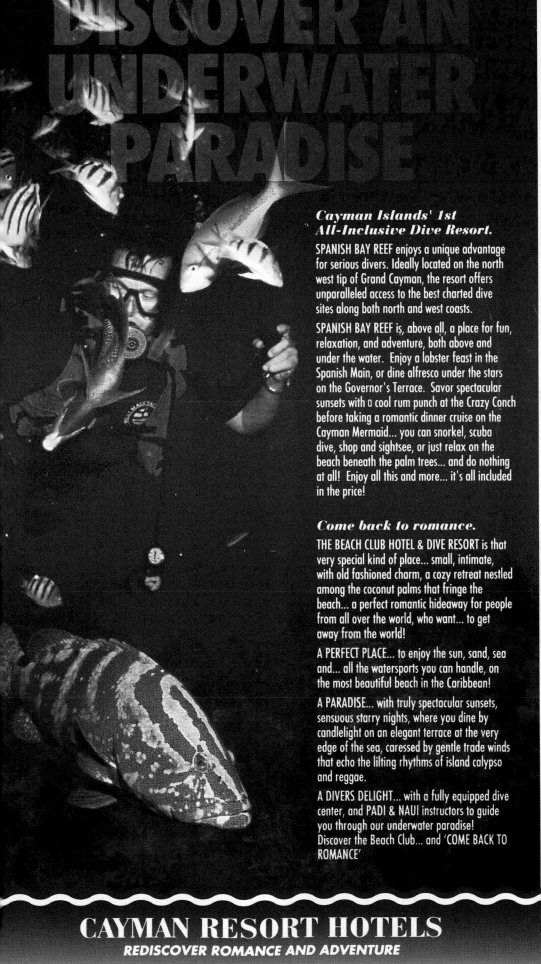

DISCOVER AN UNDERWATER PARADISE

Cayman Islands' 1st All-Inclusive Dive Resort.

SPANISH BAY REEF enjoys a unique advantage for serious divers. Ideally located on the north west tip of Grand Cayman, the resort offers unparalleled access to the best charted dive sites along both north and west coasts.

SPANISH BAY REEF is, above all, a place for fun, relaxation, and adventure, both above and under the water. Enjoy a lobster feast in the Spanish Main, or dine alfresco under the stars on the Governor's Terrace. Savor spectacular sunsets with a cool rum punch at the Crazy Conch before taking a romantic dinner cruise on the Cayman Mermaid... you can snorkel, scuba dive, shop and sightsee, or just relax on the beach beneath the palm trees... and do nothing at all! Enjoy all this and more... it's all included in the price!

Come back to romance.

THE BEACH CLUB HOTEL & DIVE RESORT is that very special kind of place... small, intimate, with old fashioned charm, a cozy retreat nestled among the coconut palms that fringe the beach... a perfect romantic hideaway for people from all over the world, who want... to get away from the world!

A PERFECT PLACE... to enjoy the sun, sand, sea and... all the watersports you can handle, on the most beautiful beach in the Caribbean!

A PARADISE... with truly spectacular sunsets, sensuous starry nights, where you dine by candlelight on an elegant terrace at the very edge of the sea, caressed by gentle trade winds that echo the lilting rhythms of island calypso and reggae.

A DIVERS DELIGHT... with a fully equipped dive center, and PADI & NAUI instructors to guide you through our underwater paradise! Discover the Beach Club... and 'COME BACK TO ROMANCE'

CAYMAN RESORT HOTELS
REDISCOVER ROMANCE AND ADVENTURE

P.O. BOX 903, GRAND CAYMAN B.W.I. RESERVATIONS: 1-800-877-3643,
SPANISH BAY REEF: (809) 949-3765, BEACH CLUB HOTEL & DIVE RESORT: (809) 949-8100

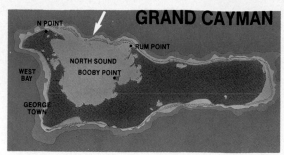

NORTH WALL

EAGLE RAY PASS

145° REEF EDGE
102° RUM POINT
282° NORTH POINT

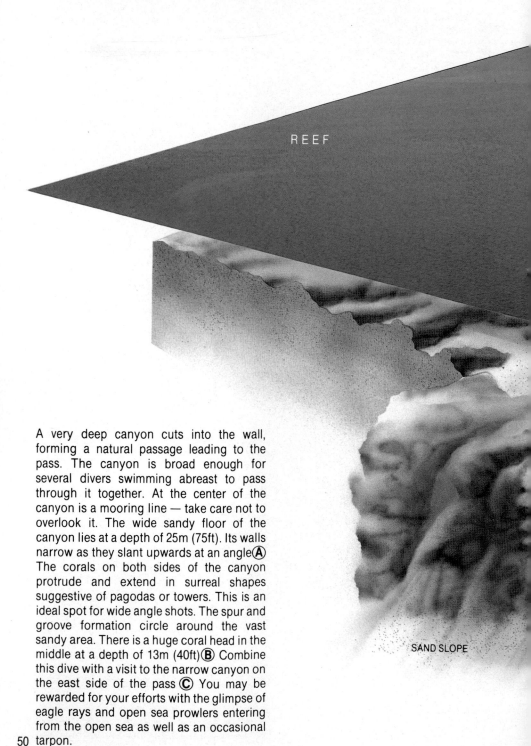

REEF

SAND SLOPE

A very deep canyon cuts into the wall, forming a natural passage leading to the pass. The canyon is broad enough for several divers swimming abreast to pass through it together. At the center of the canyon is a mooring line — take care not to overlook it. The wide sandy floor of the canyon lies at a depth of 25m (75ft). Its walls narrow as they slant upwards at an angle Ⓐ The corals on both sides of the canyon protrude and extend in surreal shapes suggestive of pagodas or towers. This is an ideal spot for wide angle shots. The spur and groove formation circle around the vast sandy area. There is a huge coral head in the middle at a depth of 13m (40ft) Ⓑ Combine this dive with a visit to the narrow canyon on the east side of the pass Ⓒ You may be rewarded for your efforts with the glimpse of eagle rays and open sea prowlers entering from the open sea as well as an occasional tarpon.

Needless to say, Eagle Ray Pass takes its name from the eminently graceful eagle rays which cruise past the open sea and the coral reef lagoon. The pass is situated directly across from the main channel. The subtle beauty of its intertwining and weaving canyons is bound to make a lasting impression.

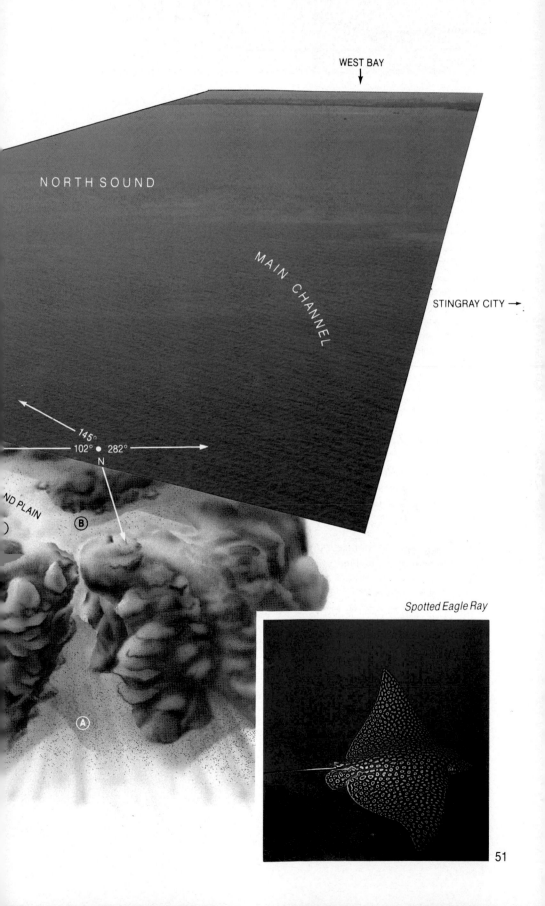

WEST BAY

NORTH SOUND

MAIN CHANNEL

STINGRAY CITY →

145°
102° ● 282° →
N

ND PLAIN

Ⓑ

Ⓐ

Spotted Eagle Ray

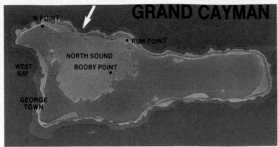

TARPON ALLEY

282° NORTH POINT
102° RUM POINT
150° WEST CHANNEL MARKER

Three major canyons radiate outwards from a central enclave **A**. These narrow, relatively shallow canyons are tarpon territory! One of them leads in the direction of the dropoff **B**, while the other two open out onto a sand plain **C**. Starting your dive from the meeting point of the three canyons allows you to scout out exactly where the resident school of tarpons is situated at a given time.

Two additional canyons lie to the west and east, and tarpons may sometimes be found here, too. The spurs lining these canyons are not particularly rich, except for the slightly higher stretch **D**, with its two caves, where species of coral flora and fauna are more abundant. Even so, any exploration of these spurs is merely incidental to the real point of

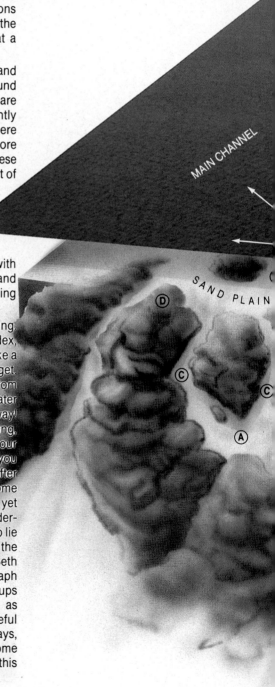

your dive—an exhilirating encounter with tarpons. The sand plain itself is broad and flat, with two prominent coral heads jutting out at the entrance to the canyons **E**.

Diving among tarpons is truly thrilling. These impressive fish (see the Fish Index, page 134) travel in large groups, and make a particularly tempting photographic target. But you will find these predators far from easy prey, as numerous underwater photographers have learnt — the hard way! Because of their burnished silver coloring, tarpons reflect and scatter the light of your flash. After shooting whole rolls of film, you may be dismayed to discover that photo after photo is marred by the same effect: some tarpons appear to be over-exposed, yet others in the same shot appear under-exposed. One way of combatting this is to lie on the canyon floor and to photograph the tarpons from beneath, a technique Beth Shelton used when shooting the photograph which accompanies this text. Close-ups demand considerable patience, as well as accurate positioning of your flash or careful exploitation of natural light. Eagle rays, turtles, jacks and snappers are among some of the other species to be found at this location.

Tarpons, a territorial species, make their home at various points off the shores of Grand Cayman, including **Bonnie's Arch** (see page 66) and, needless to say, Tarpon Alley. The latter site is also known as New Tarpon Alley to distinguish it from the original Tarpon Alley which lay off the south-western shore of the Island. It lies between two buoys on the western side of the Main Channel, very close to Stingray City. The dive described here focuses on the area surrounding the westernmost buoy, although tarpons are to be found throughout the demarcated region. Tarpon Alley is a deep dive, and may profitably be twinned with a second, shallow dive at the nearby Stingray City.

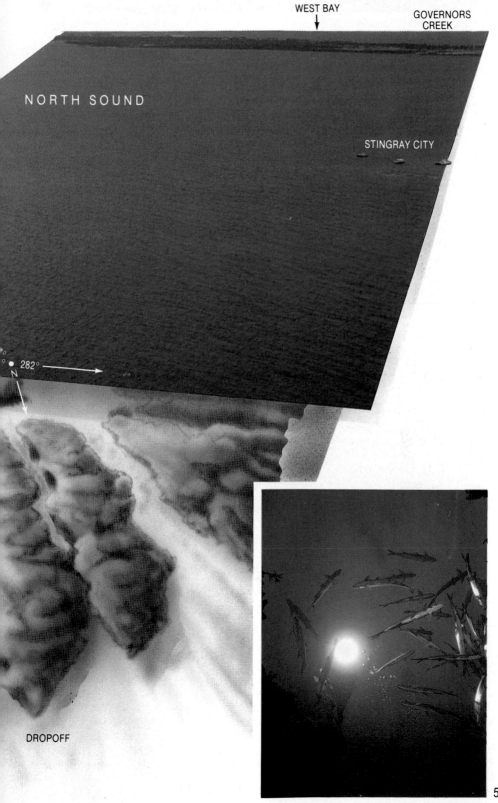

WEST BAY

GOVERNORS CREEK

NORTH SOUND

STINGRAY CITY

282°

N

DROPOFF

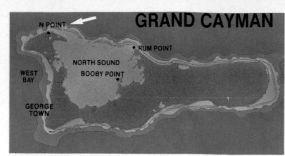

GRAND CAYMAN

NORTH WALL
BLACK FOREST

270° NORTH POINT
110° RUM POINT
125° BARKERS POINT

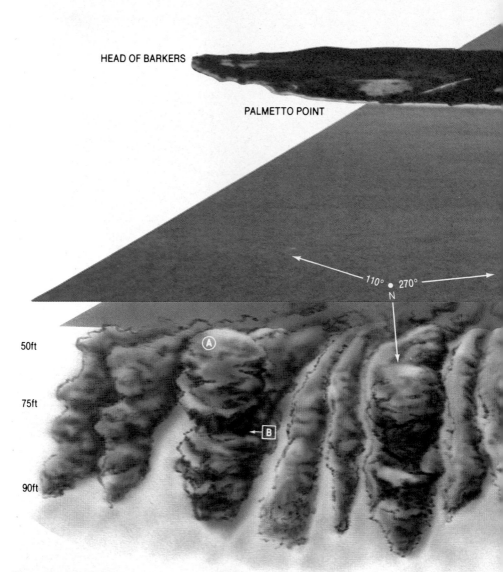

The site is characterized by three large pinnacles whose peaks, lying at roughly 17m (50ft), are all higher than the surrounding sand plain, which lies at a depth of 20m (60ft). Each pinnacle features a step or knee bearing coral outcrops that are shaped like rhinoceros horns.

Your recommended route begins at the eastern pinnacle Ⓐ—the highest of the three. It is flanked by narrow sandy canyons which lie at a moderate depth. The knee of the pinnacle is especially dense in black coral. This pinnacle is separated from the central pinnacle by three narrow canyons. The central pinnacle is wider than the first, and sports a relatively large rhino horn. A further canyon divides the central pinnacle from the last of the trio, gradually broadening into a wide sand chute B.

This site is part of the long dropoff extending from the Main Channel to North Point or Conch Point (refer also to the next site, **Ghost Mountain**, page 56). The line of the dropoff is easily discerned thanks to the accompanying fringing reef. The dropoff here is characterized by a system of large pinnacles, canyons, and sand chutes which descend from the sand plain to the base of the wall. Black Forest is rendered especially beautiful by the density of its pinnacles and canyons, and by the abundance of its black coral and gorgonians. Since no buoy formally marks this site, relatively few divers visit it.

SOUND

The mouth of the canyon is so overgrown with coral that it forms a kind of cave. A similar, but slightly deeper, cave lies in a canyon to the west of the third pinnacle. Gorgonians are very much in evidence here. Pass under the beautiful archway © into the western canyon, and continue along it as it ascends to the sand plain, before proceeding east to the mooring.

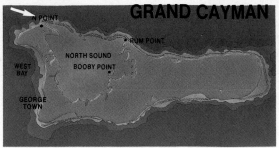

GRAND CAYMAN NORTH WALL

GHOST MOUNTAIN

181° WESTERN CORNER OF
PAPAGALLO VILLAS
128° PALMETTO POINT
240° BOATSWAINS POINT

Long spurs extend towards a slope which gradually descends to the seafloor. The Ghost Mountain or pinnacle lies at the foot of the slope, but is quite distinct from it, enabling you to circle its entire perimeter. Its base, measured from the slope, lies at a depth of 40m (120ft). Measured from the open water, it lies at a depth of 46m (140ft). The pinnacle towers up above the sandy bottom, its crest reaching a depth of 23m (70ft), which puts it almost level with the sand plain lying 22m (65ft) below the surface. Its size has been exaggerated slightly for effect in the accompanying diagram. The pinnacle resembles three mushrooms, all interlinked. A large step separates its top and bottom sections. Gorgonians and sea-fans thrive on the perpetual movement of the current here, and are large and plentiful.

A cave extends along the base of the pinnacle. Huge schools of jacks move constantly in and out of the cave, disappearing and suddenly reappearing much to the delight of divers. Do not be tempted into following them, the 40m (120ft) deep cave might be too deep for you! Two further pinnacles flank the slope. The northern one is the richer of the two, and is worth exploring in its own right. Eagle rays and the occasional shark have also been sighted in this area.

PAPAGALLO VILLAS

REEF

70ft

120ft

140ft

Approach this site from the direction of the open water, rather than making a more conventional entry from the buoy, and you will soon discover how appropriate its name really is! A giant pinnacle rises out of the depths, seeming to float in space just like a ghost mountain. This is unquestionably a unique site, offering an effortless, yet compelling dive, and a variety of subjects well suited to wide-angle photography. Ghost Mountain is located directly opposite Papagallo Condominiums. To the north lie shallow waters where the edge of the fringing reef is clearly visible.

WEST BAY

SPANISH BAY REEF

**IN FRONT OF SPANISH BAY REEF
ALL INCLUSIVE RESORT**

SPANISH BAY REEF
ALL INCLUSIVE RESORT

Proceed from the marina at Spanish Bay Reef Resort to the dive site via a sandy channel Ⓐ which widens progressively as it grows deeper. Watch out for boat traffic in the area. When you reach the coral heads, turn right (i.e., to the northwest) and you will soon arrive at the mini-wall whose structure resembles the crest of a giant breaker frozen in mid course. Together, the coral heads and the wall form an arching canyon Ⓑ. At the point where it intersects with a fissure in the wall, a new mini-canyon begins. Here you will come across a memorial tablet Ⓒ. Begin your return route now by turning towards the wall lip. A very large coral head Ⓓ is one of the more prominent landmarks along your way. It lies only a short distance from the sandy channel which leads back to the marina.

This location is great for macro

The fringing reef running along the length of the North Coast ends at North Point (Conch Point), in the region of **Ghost Mountain.** From here onwards, the general structure of the dropoff changes perceptibly. The sand plain area shrinks, the sea floor lies at shallower depths, and the dropoffs run parallel to the shore at a short distance from it. Since the dropoffs are neither as steep, nor as deep, as their North Coast counterparts, they are often termed mini-walls. All of these factors combine to make this area — **Spanish Bay** — extremely suitable for shore diving. The specific site described below lies about 110m (120 yards) off the beach of **Spanish Bay Reef Resort,** an easy swim from the shore.

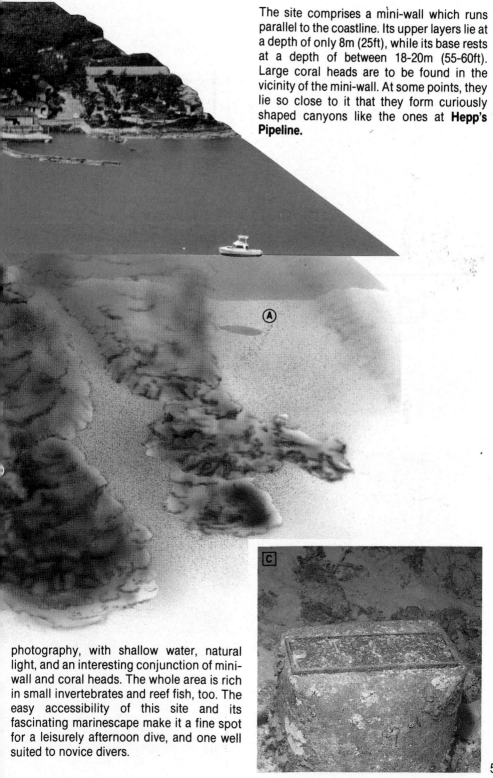

The site comprises a mini-wall which runs parallel to the coastline. Its upper layers lie at a depth of only 8m (25ft), while its base rests at a depth of between 18-20m (55-60ft). Large coral heads are to be found in the vicinity of the mini-wall. At some points, they lie so close to it that they form curiously shaped canyons like the ones at **Hepp's Pipeline.**

photography, with shallow water, natural light, and an interesting conjunction of mini-wall and coral heads. The whole area is rich in small invertebrates and reef fish, too. The easy accessibility of this site and its fascinating marinescape make it a fine spot for a leisurely afternoon dive, and one well suited to novice divers.

59

TURTLE FARM REEF

As its name suggests, Turtle Farm Reef lies just east of the Turtle Farm, a short swim from the shore. This steep mini-wall spans a depth of between 8-20m (25-60ft). It is home to a large variety of sponges, coral and other captivating macro subjects. Effluents originating from the farm provide nourishment for the many reef dwelling species here, which accounts for the very high concentration of fish at this location.

SCHOOLHOUSE REEF AND CEMETERY REEF

The area east of the Turtle Farm abounds in shallow diving sites, among them Schoolhouse and Cemetery Reefs named after adjacent onshore locations. Marine life is rich and plentiful, and the mini-wall is adorned with yellow tube sponges and basket sponges at many points. Enliven this leisurely dive by trying to find the underground tube of icy water which spews forth from a crack in the wall. Although their precise source is a mystery, such tubes are not uncommon in this area.

Brain coral and sea anemone photographed at Turtle Farm Reef

A pile of Spiny Lobsters

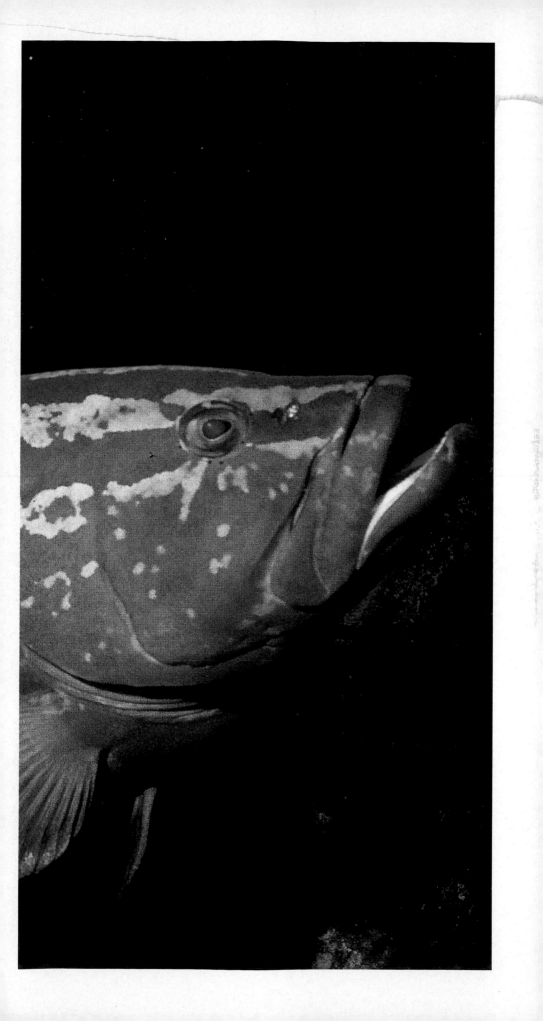

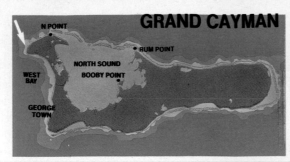

OFFSHORE FROM THE TURTLE FARM.

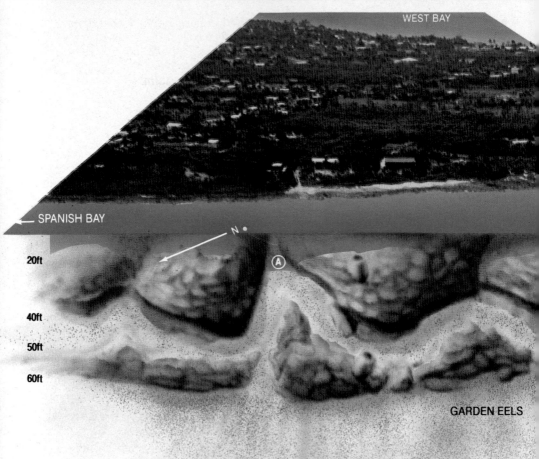

WEST BAY

← SPANISH BAY

20ft

40ft

50ft

60ft

GARDEN EELS

CORAL SLOPE

Leslie enjoying the company of an arrowhead crab

62

Hepp's Pipeline is a rather special dive site made up of two mini-walls separated from each other by a wide, flat and long sand plain located about 300m (900ft) north of Turtle Farm. It is situated very close to the shore and is demarcated by a buoy making it easy to locate. Its proximity to the shore, and the fact that the mini-walls run parallel to the coastline make Hepp's Pipeline particularly suitable for snorkeling. The actual diving area extends for about half a kilometer (a quarter of a mile).

The mooring is anchored at the entrance to a sandy canyon which cuts the wall almost in the middle Ⓐ This canyon opens out onto a wider one. Once in the water, you may choose to explore the northern or southern sections of the site. The southern option is recommended as a starting point as it is a somewhat richer dive. Following this, time permitting, proceed north.

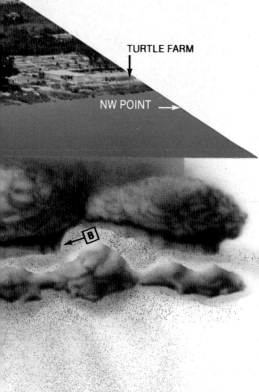

TURTLE FARM

NW POINT →

B →

Corals, sponges and gorgonians luxuriantly cover the rounded wall top. This frozen wave-like reef weaves in and out, its twisting perimeter mirrored by the huge coral heads which lie nearby. Together, the reef and coral heads appear to be the mismatching pieces of some intricate yet irregular jigsaw puzzle. This formation creates an underwater pipeline or tunnel-like structure, big enough to swim through or stand under. The combination of open sea and flat sandy ground makes for an unusual spectrum of marine life. The sand plain extends outwards about 40m (120ft) to the second mini-wall. This area then slopes down to a depth of 50m (150ft).

The reef is, in fact, a hive of activity with a thriving community of squibs and small animals — so get that macro lens shooting! Explore the big barrel sponges and rich coral life. Lobsters nestle in amongst the corals and the sandy plain is home to a huge colony of garden eels. Turtle grass grows sporadically. As most diving here is conducted over sandy ground, remember careless finning will disturb the sandy bottom.

B

THE WEST COAST

The West Coast of Grand Cayman is the second of the general diving areas covered in this book. It features two well-known, yet contrasting, diving sites: West Bay, which includes the famous Seven Mile Beach, and the area of George Town and its southern stretch.

The western region is, in fact, the most famous and popular of the Cayman diving sites. It is easily accessible to divers thanks to its relative proximity to the shore and because most hotels are situated along the West Bay beach area. The weather is usually good and the diving sites are extremely beautiful.

Anchors are obsolete since most of the diving sites are demarcated with buoys. The dive operators are familiar with the reef and treat it with particular care. Despite the caution exercised here, however, the reef has become damaged from careless finning and over-zealous photographers. No photo is worth a broken gorgonian or a smashed sponge — damage which even time may fail to heal — so be particularly cautious while swimming between canyon walls or when trying to get a good shooting angle.

The reef line at Northwest Point is actually the continuation of the North Wall which encircles the whole of Grand Cayman. It is at Northwest Point that the reef changes course, curving away from the north and drifting down towards the south. It hugs the shoreline for quite a stretch and then swerves in a more south-easterly direction. The further south the reef curves, the further away the dropoff is from the shoreline.

The southern stretch of West Bay is a huge flat sand plain with many coral heads. It is along this area, south of George Town, that dive operators conduct shore dives without boats.

To summarize, the West Coast offers a varied combination of dropoffs, a sand plain area with corals, mini-walls with intriguing caves and tunnels and, of course, wrecks. The fish are used to divers and so are quite tame and readily photographed. Grand Cayman's West Coast is truly a diver's paradise!

George Town

Seven Mile Beach

BONNIE'S ARCH
CONDOMINIUMS

A sandy ravine Ⓐ leads from the mooring to the wall. Turn right at this point, and the arch will be directly in front of you. (If there is a current, reverse the direction of your dive, as mentioned above). Although the arch looks impressively solid, with its dense living lining of corals, gorgonians and sponges, it is actually very fragile. Don't climb on it, and avoid exhaling as you swim beneath it. Your bubbles may become trapped under the arch, causing damage to its corals and sponges.

The extent of the arch makes it a perfect location for wide-angle photography, so come equipped with the right lens. The arch is literally the gateway to a large cathedral-like cavity. Here, on the sandy sea floor, you'll come across a very unusual marine reptile. Don't be alarmed, this particular crocodile Ⓑ is simply a realistic statue by

Few dive locations combine the captivating beauty and convenience which have earned Bonnie's Arch its much deserved popularity. This site lies close to the shore, well within the range of competent swimmers. Its moderate depths and kaleidoscopic population of reef fish make it attractive to snorkelers. And for the diver, there are the dual pleasures of an intricate coral archway and a resident school of tarpon.

The tarpons of Bonnie's Arch feel quite at home with divers. Approach them cautiously enough and you'll be sure to get great close ups. Note that there is often a strong current here. If you encounter it, plan to return to your boat so that you swim with the current, not against it.

Bonnie's Arch was named in memory of Bonnie Charles, a much loved diver and photographer who lived here in the sixties and seventies.

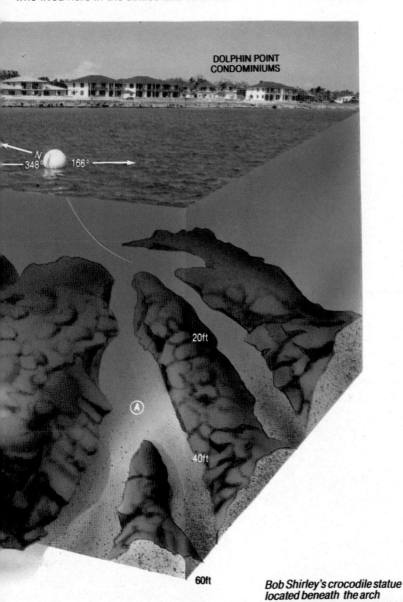

DOLPHIN POINT CONDOMINIUMS

N
— 348° 166° —

20ft

Ⓐ

40ft

60ft

Bob Shirley's crocodile statue located beneath the arch

Ⓑ

Bob Shirley. Remember, careless finning will stir up murky clouds of silt from the sandy bottom

Some massive barrel sponges, up to 3m (8ft) in diameter, are to be found on the wall in front of the arch Ⓒ, unless dislodged by recent storms. The tarpon are generally located in the 'cathedral' although they sometimes wander off to the grotto which lies a little to the north Ⓓ. Apart from tarpons, you will find colorful reef-dwellers including angel fish, filefish and triggers.

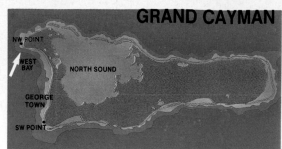

ORANGE CANYON

336° NW POINT
168° SW POINT

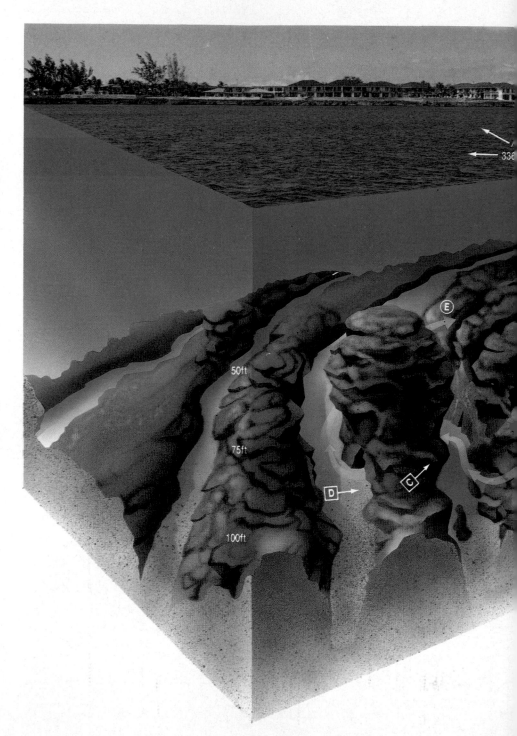

Orange Canyon is the deepest, northernmost site in the West Bay series. This magnificent dive is located relatively close to the beach off the Bonnie's Arch condominium complex, right opposite the NW point. No prizes for guessing the source of its name – the cluster of large orange elephant-ear sponges found on one side of the pinnacle here is breathtaking! Once again, the reef topography follows the familiar pattern of canyons which slope down from shallow to deep water.

The diving area is concentrated mainly around the large coral pinnacle and the cave at its base. It is in easy reach of the nearby mooring, so you'll be able to conduct a leisurely dive. Don't hurry. If you plan to photograph, set up your shots to maximize the dramatic impact of the huge orange sponges! But remember, there is often a strong current here.

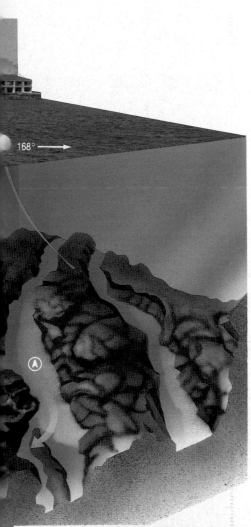

168° ⟶

Ⓐ

The mooring pin lies a little to the east of the dive site. Once in the water, look for the canyon leading straight to the dropoff Ⓐ. Follow it to the dropoff, then turn right Ⓑ towards the pinnacle which should now be very prominent. On entering the short canyon which circles it, you should be able to observe the first of the orange elephant ear sponges Ⓒ. There's little need to point out just how photogenic a spot this is! At the base of the pinnacle, there is a cave which passes through to the far side Ⓓ. Although the cave is narrow, you can negotiate it fairly comfortably as long as you don't plan on turning around. Above the cave is a small crevice, permanent home to a giant crab which may, or may not, be visible. If you prefer to bypass the cave, circle the pinnacle in order to complete the suggested route or turn in the opposite direction towards a short canyon opening out onto a cave Ⓔ. Despite the fact that the cave is a dead-end, it is worth investigating. If you are diving here during the summer, you will almost certainly find a school of silverside — tarpons' favorite prey. There can be no finer souvenir of this particular dive than a photograph shot from inside the cave looking out through a moving cloud of silversides!

Apart from the coral and sponges, the usual reef-dwellers abound here, particularly large and rather curious angel fish. At the beginning of spring, you might come across a solitary tarpon. Its presence in this unusual location is not hard to explain. It is most probably a spy sent by the permanent school at Bonnie's Arch, some 45m (50 yards) away, to scout out the silverside situation.

Ⓓ

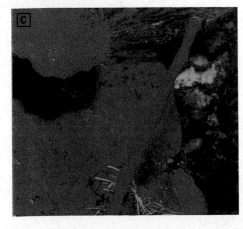

Ⓒ

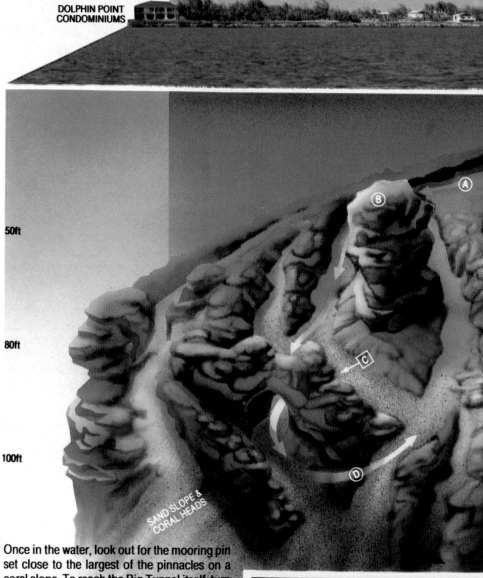

GRAND CAYMAN WEST BAY
BIG TUNNEL

321° NW POINT
169° SW POINT

DOLPHIN POINT
CONDOMINIUMS

50ft

80ft

100ft

SAND SLOPE &
CORAL HEADS

Once in the water, look out for the mooring pin
set close to the largest of the pinnacles on a
coral slope. To reach the Big Tunnel itself, turn
in the opposite direction (A) towards an
isolated pinnacle (B). Its size has been
exaggerated in the drawing—in reality it is a
little smaller. Enter the canyon from its northern
end, and it will lead you to a coral head where
two humps mushroom out. The Big Tunnel is
located beneath it [C]. This is a wide, high cave
with a flat, even artificial-looking, sandy floor. It
twists to the left and opens out onto a short
canyon leading to the dropoff. At this point, you
will be at a depth of more than 30m (100 ft), so
don't be tempted to continue along the length

70

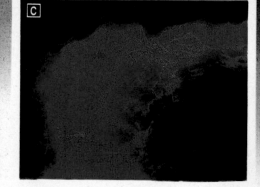

The Big Tunnel is one of the most challenging sites on your West Bay diving itinerary, situated in an area furrowed by spiralling canyons. Dive it only if you have the experience needed to negotiate its depths, ranging between 26-30m (80-100 ft), and its sometimes tricky passages through caves and canyons. This is a large location and can be divided into two or three smaller sites. The dive plan recommended here covers the site as a whole, and is based on a bottom time of 20 minutes. So allocate your time strictly, being especially careful about the length of time you spend at the deepest levels. The focus of the dive is the large cave or 'Big Tunnel' for which the site is named. Its dimensions are impressive even in a region as rich in canyons and caves as this one. The Big Tunnel is wide enough to accommodate three to four divers swimming abreast.

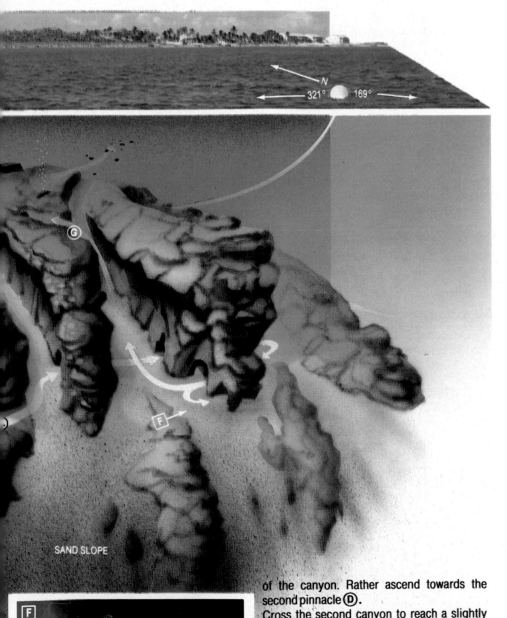

SAND SLOPE

of the canyon. Rather ascend towards the second pinnacle Ⓓ.

Cross the second canyon to reach a slightly deeper one Ⓔ, where you will find an elongated pinnacle with a cave at its base. Pass through the cave to the large pinnacle and its network of interconnecting caves F. Great photo opportunities abound here, against the background of a rich variety of sponges, gorgonians and black corals. If you have time left, stop off at another small cave Ⓖ. Nested like a chinese-box inside it is an even smaller cave, a dead-end with no exit other than a tiny fissure in the roof.

71

BIG DIPPER AND LITTLE TUNNEL

These two very popular locations are situated close enough to one another to be treated as one dive site. At first glance, the Big Dipper might be taken simply for one of the large pinnacles that dominate the West Bay Wall. But, as its name suggests, it displays a very unusual feature: a large "black hole" which snakes through its hollow center, and which can be dived to a depth of 33m (100ft) or 40m (120ft). The deeper dive is best attempted only under the direction of a local dive master. Little Tunnel lies some 27m (30 yards) east of Big Dipper, and is so named for the tunnel close to the mooring that leads divers out onto the wall. To the west of the tunnel is a large pinnacle complete with gorgonians, colorful sponges and a very large brown barrel sponge.

SANDCHUTE

This wall dive situated in the northern section of Seven Mile Beach is dominated by a massive river of sand, 100m (300ft) wide, which avalanches its way downwards between huge coral walls and eventually plunges to a depth of over 115m (345ft). The 20m (60ft) high walls on either side are impressive in themselves, and extend for a distance of approximately 33m (100ft). Unfortunately, some of the largest basket sponge formations here were destroyed by Hurricane Gilbert in 1988. Even so, the Sandchute offers much to interest the diver.

ROUND ROCK

Lying to the west of **Trinity Caves**, Round Rock is a small pinnacle pulled back into a coral canyon at 27m (80ft). You will find it easy to swim all the way around the pinnacle. As you do so, look out for the wealth of sponges, sea plume gorgonians, and black coral trees that cover its sides.

MITCH MILLER'S REEF

This reef is named for the famous bandleader of the fifties and sixties who used to own a small house looking out onto this shallow dive site. Many large coral heads grooved with twisting tunnels and swim-throughs typify Mitch Miller's Reef.

NEPTUNE'S WALL

Situated east of **Trinity**, this site consists of a gradual sloping dropoff. A large coral head and a gorgonian and black coral encrusted swim-through are the major features of this site.

It takes two to tango - Roni and a stingray.
(left) A Diamond Blenny with its favorite shelter, the sea anemone

73

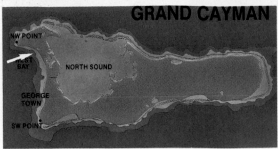

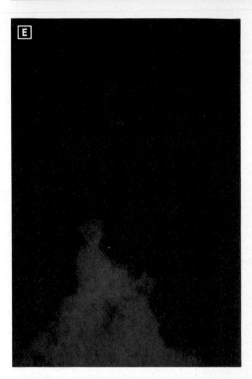

NORTH SOUND

ANCHORAGE VIEW

The dive begins in 17m (50ft) of water. Set out from the cave entrance, 12m (35ft) from the base of the mooring, and take the ravine which lies to your left (i.e. to the east) as you approach. After swimming under a coral arch (or saddle) midway through the ravine, you will come to a fork. Take the left-hand passage Ⓐ, as the other leads to a dead end. The floor of the ravine drops gradually and bends several times as it brings you out onto the wall.

At the exit of the cave, you will see the dropoff in front of you, and a superb coral pinnacle to the right Ⓑ. This dramatic combination is ideal camera material. The beautifully formed pinnacle extends to within 18m (55ft) of the surface. Your exploration of the pinnacle will take you to another ravine Ⓒ, filled with black coral trees, levelling out at 33m (100ft). Exercise caution on leaving it as you might tend to follow the wall down beyond safe depth limits. Swimming along the wall will bring you to the second of Trinity's major ravines Ⓓ, which affords easy passage back to the entrance to the system and on to the anchor line.

One of Grand Cayman's most famous and most beautiful dives, Trinity is located in the West Bay Bight some 450m (500 yards) offshore. Its fame dates back to the early seventies when it first began to attract divers. Since that time, scarcely a day has gone by without enthusiasts diving this site.

Trinity consists of three long ravines running parallel to one another in the direction of the dropoff. Although easily accessible, the ravines are narrow enough in places to be termed caves. Occasional saddles of coral are to be found at the roof of the ravines at some points.

Note: The caves and canyons are actually very narrow (see photograph) but are slightly wider in the illustration in order to show their structure.

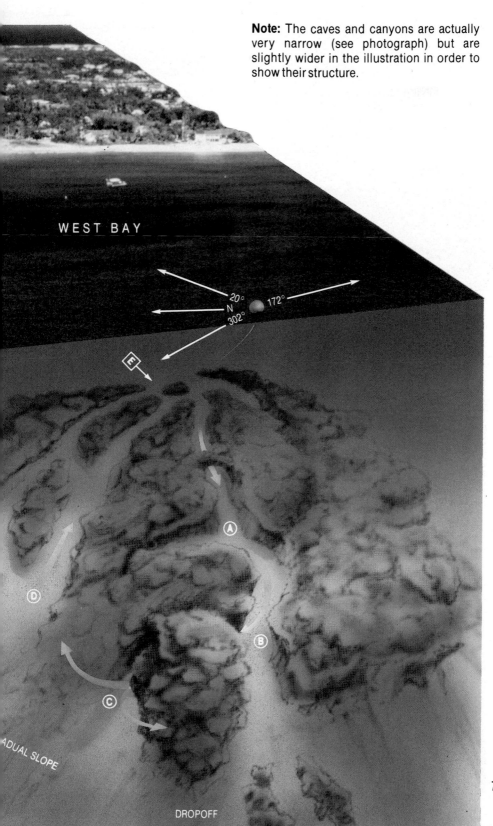

WEST BAY

20°
N
302°
172°

E

A

D

B

C

ADUAL SLOPE

DROPOFF

SPANISH ANCHOR

This coral reef is located about 1 km (3/4 mile) northwest of the public beach. The coral finger formation expands westward in a typical West Bay shallow reef formation.

The site's main attraction is an antique 2.5m (8 ft) Spanish anchor which lies at a depth of 13.5 m (40 ft), making it a popular site for a second dive. There is no evidence to prove that the anchor is Spanish or to indicate which ship it once belonged to, but like most site names in the Caymans, this site has its roots in the past, and the name has stuck.

The anchor is not easy to find, since it is almost completely encrusted by coral. Careful scrutiny of the accompanying photograph shows the location of the anchor's large ring as it appears underwater. First look for a brown barrel sponge on the top of the central coral ridge. Slightly below it is a short, shallow channel and in it lies the anchor.

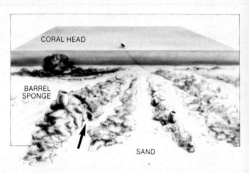

Myriad friendly Grey and French Angelfish inhabit the spot and will keep you company throughout the dive.

AQUARIUM REEF

Aquarium Reef is often considered the prettiest of the shallow dive sites on the west side of the island, and is similar in configuration to most of the others. It is a spur and groove formation with fingers of coral jutting out from a continuous reef which runs the length of Seven Mile Beach. The top of the formation lies between 10-12m (30-35ft) sloping down to the 17m (50ft) level where the coral fingers meet the sand.

True to its name, Aquarium is populated by large numbers of very tame fish which are happy to eat from a diver's hand. Expect sergeant majors, yellow-tailed snappers, french and gray angels and Nassau groupers, all easily coaxed to pose by the offer of a tidbit.

Small coral heads, yellow tube sponges and barrel sponges are also to be found here. A stand of pillar coral, unusual for the west side of the island, is only a short swim to the south.

As with the majority of the shallow spur and groove reefs, this site is used as the second dive of a two tank, or as a shallow afternoon drive. It also makes an excellent night dive.

The outstanding pillar coral at the Aquarium reef

THE WRECK OF THE ORO VERDE

The Oro Verde just before sinking

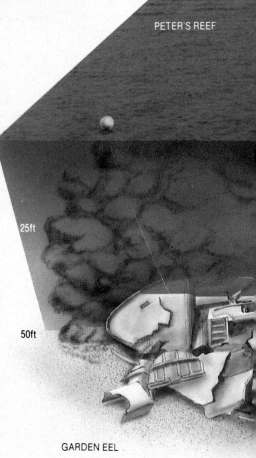

PETER'S REEF

25ft

50ft

GARDEN EEL

Two moorings are attached to the *Oro Verde*, one at the bow and another at the stern. Be careful about penetrating the wreck which is made hazardous by sharp metal and confined spaces. As a general rule, only enter if you can see the exit.

The wreck, a veritable classroom for novice underwater photographers, is home to a vast array of friendly reef fish with all the panache of professional models, along with ocean-going species such as horse-eyed jacks and sea bream. The *Oro Verde* also provides an occasional home for large jewfish, eels and barracuda. Fish feeding is a popular pastime, but beware — the fish are voracious and can surprise the unwary diver. The kaleidoscope of colorful marine life here guarantees great enjoyment for fish feeder and photographer alike.

Shoreward of the wreck is an interesting shallow reef, depth 12-17m (35-50ft), known as Peter's Reef. Navigating this particular site is very easy. Looking westward into the sandy area beyond the *Oro Verde,* you will see a colony of garden eels half-hidden in their burrows (see the Fish Index, page 136).

Enjoying a reputation as one of the most popular wreck dives in the world, the *Oro Verde* was purchased at the end of her life by Bob Soto and a group of dive operators on Grand Cayman to become the island's first man-made dive site, having been sunk for that purpose in April 1980. The 63m (189ft) wreck, torn into several large pieces by occasional winter storms, lies scattered on a sandy bottom in 17m (50ft) of water off the Holiday Inn on Seven Mile Beach. The *Oro Verde* is sister ship to the *USS Pueblo* captured by the North Koreans as a spy ship.

NORTH SOUND

HOLIDAY INN

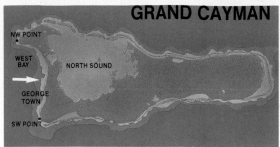

GRAND CAYMAN WEST BAY
ROYAL PALMS
LEDGE

58° HYATT TOWER
180° SW POINT
334° NW POINT

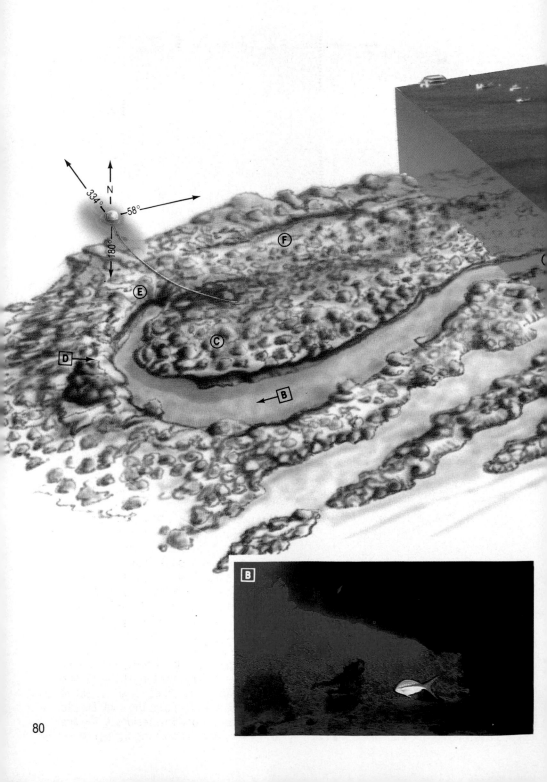

Following normal canyon structure in the Caymans, the spurs and grooves of the Royal Palms Ledge lead away from shore, but where elsewhere these generally end in the dropoff, the horseshoe shaped tunnel with its unusual overhang circles around towards the shore and then comes to a dead end. The site looks artificial; the "frozen wave" formation of the overhang and fine white sand along the sea floor seem to have been formed by a bulldozer and not naturally. The site is located directly in front of the new Radisson hotel at the southern end of Seven Mile Beach. It was named after the Royal Palms Hotel which was destroyed in a fire in 1987.

HYATT REGENCY
HOTEL

The canyon starts at a depth of 10 m (35 ft) Ⓐ and is deepest at the bend, where it reaches 17 m (50 ft). The overhang is at its greatest width closest to the bend, almost completely covering the canyon to form a tunnel. This is also the widest point: several divers can swim abreast here Ⓑ. The coral heads covering this area from the outside are more developed Ⓒ and this is an ideal site for photographs since air bubbles released under the overhang make their way through the rock Ⓓ as they rise. The canyon continues as if to turn back to shore, and then suddenly comes to an end Ⓔ. There is another shallow canyon slightly to the north which seems to be a continuation of the half-circle, and is also worth a visit. Ⓕ Both day and nighttime sea creatures may be found at the site, for there is plenty of light as well as dark shadow under the overhang. The site is fairly shallow, and is suitable for a second dive or an afternoon dive.

While diving Royal Palms Ledge, fin carefully as you move through the tunnel, for the fine sand is easily disturbed and a single thoughtless move can ruin the dive. Due to the multitude of nocturnal residents, the site is also a very popular spot for night dives.   81

FISHEYE FANTASY (Also called Ashton's Wall)

A deep site between **Sandchute** and **Trinity Caves**, this dive comprises three beautiful pinnacles close together. All three are easily included in one dive. A great spot for photography.

CARIBBEAN CLUB SANDCHUTE

As its name suggests, this deep site is found offshore from the Caribbean Club on the central portion of Seven Mile Beach. The dive comprises a river of sand between two low reefs. The incline is very gradual luring the diver to depths of over 40m (120ft) before falling away over the wall. Watch your depth at the deeper end of the chute to avoid breaking your profile.

EAGLE'S NEST

Beneath the mooring the depth is around 17m (50ft), just 4.5m (5 yards) away the vertical wall plunges into the abyss. A dive along the sheer wall is highlighted by an overhang under which is a massive black coral tree. Beside the overhang is an enormous brown barrel sponge. A great dive for those who want to float like an eagle over the blue.

SOTO'S REEF

The position of this reef, found directly across from the Lobster Pot and Bob Soto's Dive Center on the north side of George Town Harbor, make it one of the most famous shallow dive sites in Grand Cayman. Its round coral heads, topped with a filigree of staghorn and elkhorn coral formations, lie less than 2m (6ft) below the surface — hence its popularity with snorkelers. Divers will want to venture into the narrow passageways between the coral head clusters.

GEORGE TOWN HARBOR →

BOB SOTO'S
DIVING CENTER

SOTO'S REEF

Nassau Grouper, photographed at the Oro Verde
The head of a Smooth Trunkfish

THE WRECK OF THE KIRK PRIDE

The wreck of the *Kirk Pride* is undoubtedly one of the most spectacular — and most unconventional — wreck dives in the world, lying as it does at a depth of 267m (800ft)! Understandably, diving this site takes some rather specialized equipment in the form of one of two, 1-atmosphere, 1000ft-rated submarines operated by Research Submersibles Limited. You don't need any prior experience for this dive. In fact, you don't even have to be a Scuba diver! The submersibles, PC 1203 and PC 1802, take two passengers together with a professional pilot on a breathtaking, personalized dive beyond the depths of sport diving. You and your fellow traveler sit side by side in front of a large domed viewport, 1m (3ft) in diameter, perfect ringside seat offering an unparalleled view and marvellous photographic opportunities.

These two photographs were shot at a depth of 170m (500ft) using the submersible's quartz lights

Orange sea-fan, Micella guadalupensis, *about 1m (3ft) across*

Great West Indian sea-lily, Cenocrinus asterius, *up to 1m (3ft) tall*

GEORGE TOWN

THE WRECK OF THE KIRK PRIDE

OFFSHORE GEORGE TOWN

SOUTH SOUND

RUNWAY

THE SUBMERSIBLE PC 1203

← N

The submersible begins its descent facing the wall, whose proportions relative to it are nothing short of gargantuan! Each passing second augments the feeling of awe that possesses you, to crescendo as you finally come face to face with the *Kirk Pride* herself. At 170m (500ft), you encounter a thermocline where the water is cooler and the visibility, with available light, increases to about 133m (400ft). This incredible clarity continues, even at 267m (800ft), where the entire 60m (180ft) of the *Kirk Pride* and the surrounding area can be viewed with no lights on. The wrecked freighter is perched upright on a ledge, wedged solidly against huge carbonate blocks called haystacks. Unique creatures of the depths inhabit these haystacks: delicate branching corals, dazzling red sea-fans, and stalked crinoids which stand up to 1m (3ft) tall.

After exploring the wreck and surrounding pinnacles, the submersible starts its slow ascent up the Cayman wall. At the 150m (450ft) level, you will begin to notice an increase in colorful, thickly encrusted sponges. Another 33m (100ft) up the wall, and you are in the heart of the sponge belt.

KIRK PRIDE

HAYSTACKS

The wreck of the *Kirk Pride* lies directly opposite George Town. The submersible is anchored to a buoy above the wall in the region of the pleasure cruisers, a short Zodiac trip from the shore. The dive consists of two parts. Its first, deep leg features the wreck at a stupendous depth of 267m (800ft). On its second leg, you will pause to survey the interesting deep-sea creatures of the sponge belt located on the sheer wall between 67 and 150m (200-450ft).

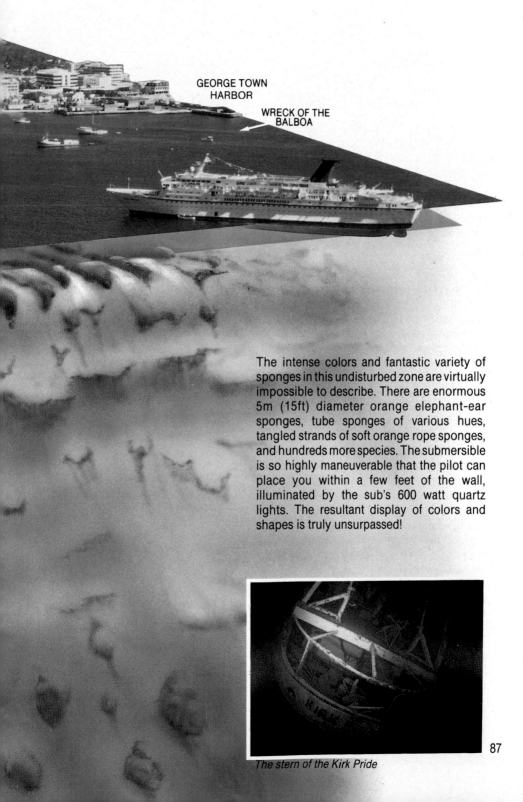

GEORGE TOWN
HARBOR

WRECK OF THE
BALBOA

The intense colors and fantastic variety of sponges in this undisturbed zone are virtually impossible to describe. There are enormous 5m (15ft) diameter orange elephant-ear sponges, tube sponges of various hues, tangled strands of soft orange rope sponges, and hundreds more species. The submersible is so highly maneuverable that the pilot can place you within a few feet of the wall, illuminated by the sub's 600 watt quartz lights. The resultant display of colors and shapes is truly unsurpassed!

The stern of the Kirk Pride

87

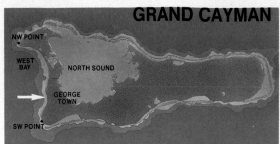

GEORGE TOWN

THE WRECK OF THE BALBOA

AT THE ENTRANCE TO GEORGE TOWN HARBOR

←—N

REEF

BOILER ROOM

BOW

Diving here usually takes place at weekends when the traffic of visiting tourist liners ceases. On weekdays, convoys of motor boats transporting tourists to Grand Cayman pass directly over the site as they ply the route between the tourist liners anchored outside the harbor and the shore. Apart from this drawback, the *Balboa* is easily accessible and easily photographed using natural light at this shallow depth. Given these conditions, its popularity with novice divers is understandable — but even veterans insist on returning to explore the many fascinations of the wreck. The *Balboa* also ranks as a prime site for night dives.

The fragments of the wreck fan out from east to west. Your first reaction to them might well be one of disappointment. True, it is possible to take in the entire site in a matter of minutes. But slow and careful exploration here will be amply rewarded as the wreckage teems with marine life. You may even enter some of the larger fragments, using them as props to stage some extraordinary underwater photographs.

The pyramid of the *Balboa*'s upturned bow marks the western extremity of the site. Next to it lie fragments of the hull and deck. Moving eastwards, you will encounter two large chunks of wreckage just south of the boiler room which looms prominently out of the sand. Continue in the direction of the harbor to reach a large belt of scattered debris reminiscent of an underwater junkyard. Here you will find the engine, axle and propeller. Immediately behind them rests the stern — one of the wreck's most photogenic areas.

This famous dive is an immensely popular site, still compelling in spite of the fact that the *Balboa* is more wreckage strewn on the sea floor than wreck! This small freighter, a lumber-carrier, sank at the entrance to George Town harbor during a devastating hurricane in 1932. The remains of the *Balboa* were subsequently dynamited since they posed a real danger to shipping in the area. The twisted metal left by the blast lies scattered in about 8m (25ft) of water close to the harbor's main pier. As a matter of interest, the freighter's cargo of wood was retrieved, and was used in the construction of the small church that stands opposite the southern tip of the harbor.

Note that proportions have been altered slightly in the accompanying diagram, in the manner of a wide-angled shot, the better to describe the site.

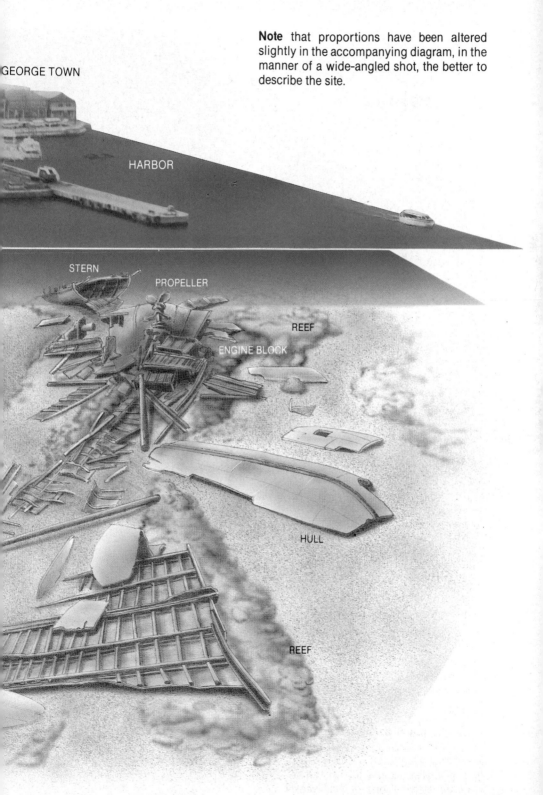

GEORGE TOWN

HARBOR

STERN

PROPELLER

REEF

ENGINE BLOCK

HULL

REEF

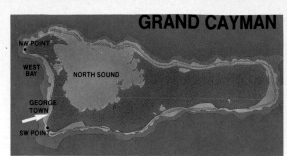

GRAND CAYMAN

NW POINT

WEST BAY

NORTH SOUND

GEORGE TOWN

SW POINT

GEORGE TOWN

EDEN ROCK & DEVIL'S GROTTO

IN FRONT OF EDEN ROCK DIVE SHOP

←GEORGE TOWN

EDEN ROC

←N

10ft   10ft

25ft

40ft

35ft

EDEN ROCK

Enter the water near the Eden Rock Dive Shop where your equipment can be readied and you can simply walk into the water. You can save air by snorkeling out to the dive site since it's only a 140m (150 yards) swim from shore to the buoys that mark the site, protecting divers below from speedboats and waterskiers. These buoys are visible from the shore and are clearly apparent in the aerial photograph.

The sea floor is sandy and covered with small coral outcrops, rocks, and sea-fans until you reach the large coral heads. The rocks become more and more frequent until they form a miniwall. Past this the sea floor is sandy, but level and cleaner.

As you approach the sand gully Ⓐ, decide which site is to be explored first: turn right (north) for Eden Rock or left (south) to Devil's Grotto. Light penetrates some of the caves from above while others are completely dark, so we recommend bringing along a flashlight.

These two popular dive sites lie in close proximity to each other and are accessible from the Eden Rock Diving Center. They are directly offshore and an easy swim or snorkel away. Located on the south side of Hog Sty Bay (George Town Harbor), they are also not far from town. The coral heads are located in fairly shallow water, making the site highly popular and frequently crowded with divers and snorkelers alike. Since the attraction of the dive is its amazing labyrinth of tunnels, they appear here in a cutaway view to show them in all their intricacy. Although Eden Rock and Devil's Grotto are separated only by a sand gully, we recommend diving each site separately in order to see as much as possible. The two dives can be done one after the other since they are relatively shallow.

VE SHOP

15ft

25ft

Ⓐ

35ft

40ft

50ft

DEVIL'S GROTTO

The best camera prey here are Glassy Sweepers who love the darkness of the tunnels. This is an excellent site to photograph these and other nocturnal fish, and a night dive by flashlight is highly recommended. This is a favorite tarpon haunt in the springtime, although there are always a few around throughout the year.

Take your time in the grottos and don't try to cover everything in a few minutes. Don't forget to explore the outside of the coral heads also. If you become confused and lose your sense of direction in the caves, remember that as a rule, they run lengthwise from the shore. Don't try to swim up and out — just follow the cave to its end and you'll be able to find your bearings.

The grotto and its residents, the Glassy Sweepers

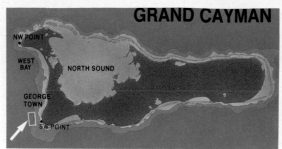

GRAND CAYMAN GEORGE TOWN

PARROT'S REEF
SUNSET REEF
WALDO'S REEF
EAGLE RAY ROCK

The entire stretch of coast south of George Town, bounded by Eden Rock on the one end and Northwest Point on the other, is actually one long reef with large coral heads rising up from the sandy sea floor. The proximity of George Town and the abundance of highly professional dive resorts along the coastal road combine to lend this area its special character, and make it especially suited to shore diving. Many of the dive operations here feature dedicated dive clubs as well as luxurious accommodation. Guests enjoy the convenience of being able to dive off their very doorsteps! Needless to say, most resorts also offer the option of diving at more distant locations on the island.

A number of sites along the reef are worth singling out in particular:

PARROT'S REEF

The broad expanse of Parrot's Reef is cleft by a series of shallow sandy canyons, with depths ranging from 7-15m (20-45ft). It is best approached from the nearby Parrot's Landing, where you can assemble your equipment and enter the water using the ladder conveniently positioned off the deck of the landing. Initially, the sand-bottomed sea floor is broken up by

NORTH SOUND

EDEN ROCK DIVE SHOP

←GEORGE TOWN

PARROT LANDING

DEVIL'S GROTTO

PARROT REEF

←N

small, relatively sparse coral heads, but these become ever larger and more dense with increased depth. To the west lie two canyons surrounded by particularly rich coral heads. If, on the other hand, you proceed in a northerly direction, you will soon reach **Devil's Grotto.** Immediately behind the pair of canyons, the ocean floor levels out and a large outcrop of isolated coral heads stands in sharp contrast to the background of glimmering white sand. Some 20m (60ft) further on lies the wreck of the *Anna Marie.* This 8m (25ft) long vessel is the most recent of Grand Cayman's wrecks, having sunk in stormy weather in October 1987. Previous to this, the diminutive tug served as a support vessel for the Atlantis submarine. Now it is home to an inquisitive Moray Eel and a variety of tiny reef creatures. Still on the subject of eels, a colony of Garden Eels is located adjacent to the wreck. Be prepared for the fact that this site lies 190m (200 yards) from Parrot's Landing, so don't risk fatigue after a long dive by poor planning.

SUNSET REEF

Visitors to Sunset House Resort need little introduction to Sunset Reef, an extremely popular dive site located within swimming distance of the resort's pier. Apart from hotel guests, Nassau and Black Groupers, Moray Eels, Pufferfish, Yellowtail Snappers and Sergeant Majors frequent the reef, which also features hard coral, sponges and gorgonians of all shapes and sizes. This is an especially good site for close-up photography and for night dives.

EAGLE RAY ROCK

This dramatic wall dive is situated on the southwestern extremity of Grand Cayman's west side. One of its highlights is a large L-shaped canyon with vertical sides rising to a height of 10m (30ft). The canyon is very narrow, and may be negotiated in single-file only. Entering the canyon from its shoreward end, you will see orange elephant-ear sponges in addition to the black coral trees and sea-fans which adorn the canyon walls. The site takes its name from local Eagle Rays which may often be observed as they wind their way gracefully along the dropoff at this point.

SUNSET HOUSE

SUNSET REEF

WALDO'S REEF

WALDO'S REEF

This shallow shore dive site lies some 100m (300ft) off Coconut Harbor Resort. Its chief attraction is Waldo himself, a 2m (6ft) long Green Moray eel! Be sure also to meet Bugsy and Blacky, a pair of resident Black Grouper, and the fearless Snaggletooth, a Barracuda whose curiosity knows no bounds. The reef itself is rich in sponges, hard coral and gorgonians, and also features some interesting coral caves.

Petting the famous Waldo

CAYMAN BRAC

CAYMAN BRAC

Cayman Brac and Little Cayman are Grand Cayman's sister islands and are actually two flat summits in the underwater Cayman Ridge range. While the Grand Cayman and Little Cayman islands are almost completely flat, the topography of Cayman Brac is unusually different.

The 19km (12 mile) long, 3.2km (2 mile) wide island slopes upwards from west to east. Sheer cliffs ring both sides of the eastern tip of the island, tapering off westwards where the island is low lying and truly flat. On the island's southern side the cliff edge is quite close to the sea, with only a 200m (217 yard) strip of beach at its widest point. The beach is wider (500m - 540 yards) on the island's northern side, and most of the human settlement is located here. The sheer cliffs on the island's eastern tip plunge directly into the sea and there is practically no beach. These bluffs rise almost directly out of the water to a height of 48m (140ft).

These two photographs show the contrast between the flat west Cayman Brac landscape near the airport and The Bluff as it spills into the sea on the island's eastern end

CAYMAN BRAC

The island's two main roads run along the beach under the cliffs and make for a fascinating sightseeing drive. On one side there is the sea and the beach, while on the other the sheer cliff face covered with a jungle of intertwining cacti. The cliff face is bisected by caves and canyons which are worth exploring in their own right. Another road cuts across the island's midsection, connecting the two main roads.

The island's airport is located on the flat western tip. The landing strip is paved and there is a control tower and a new, spacious terminal building. The hotels and dive resorts are located in this area, as are the main dive sites. Among these are two dive centers which are considered the Cayman's most comfortable and luxurious: airconditioned rooms, diving equipment, photo processing and rental, restaurants and swimming pools, tennis courts, etc. - an ideal holiday spot with every amenity a diver on vacation might need (see the Dive Service Guidelines page 187 for details).

Most dives are in the western tip area and involve only a short ride north or south on excellently equipped modern boats. The guides know the sites well; most are marked with official buoys. Boats also make the 50 minute trip to Little Cayman from here, an excursion usually consisting of an entire day of diving (3 or 4 dives) with lunch on board.

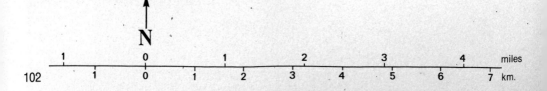

Topographically, the dive sites include characteristic Caymanian walls and dropoffs, but Cayman Brac is better known for its sand chutes: tremendous rivers of sand which pour over the wall and disappear into the blue depths. There are also plenty of sites suitable for snorkelers or shallow dives.

Relatively speaking, there are fewer divers on Cayman Brac than on Grand Cayman, and although there may not be as many tame fish, the variety and quantity of marine life is plentiful and virtually unmolested.

There are, without a doubt, plenty of dive sites in the waters around Cayman Brac that have not yet been fully explored. This chapter describes only four very popular sites on the northwestern side of the island. For general information, the Island's other well known sites are indicated on the map.

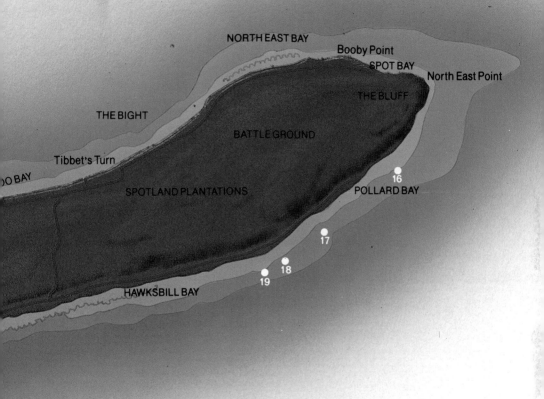

CAYMAN BRAC DIVE SITES

- ■ Detailed site description with diagram
- ★ General site description without diagram
- ● Well-known site

CAYMAN BRAC NORTH SIDE

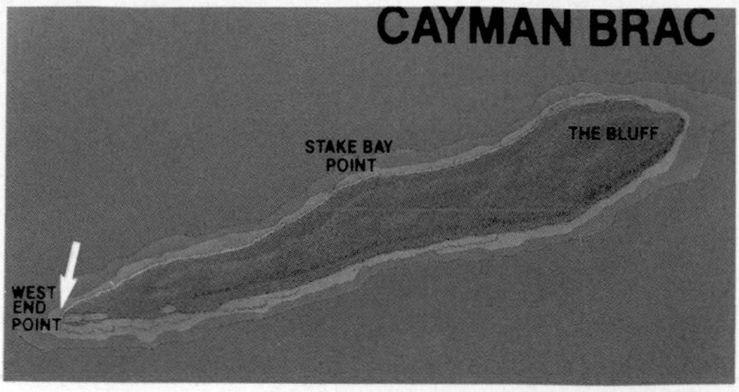
STAKE BAY POINT
THE BLUFF
WEST END POINT

AIRPORT WALL

110° END OF ROAD
180° WEST END POINT

DICK SESSINGER'S BAY
CHANNEL BAY
RUNWAY
A
60ft
90ft

D

Start your dive at the eastern, narrow canyon that drops steeply to the base of the wall. Turn left (west) under the overhang created by the pinnacle Ⓐ and swim along the crack. The crack is the dividing line between the sheer drop from the wall lip and the gentler, but still steep slope covered with coral and patches of white sand.

Located right over the western point of the island, at the beginning of the runway, the Airport Wall site is the most western dive site with the characteristic combination of walls and sand chutes, a Cayman Brac trademark. Note in the diagram the clearly delineated crack running along the upper part of the wall, which, although disappearing at times, always reappears a little further along the wall.

Continue on to the second interesting area at the site's center, where the crack has formed a wide, flat step which opens into a cave Ⓑ. Over the time, pure white sand has steadily collected in this flat area, forming a mini sand plain. The wall is punctured by a wide, sandy canyon whose floor is littered with corals, which is almost a sand chute Ⓒ. Begin your ascent here; there is plenty to see along the way in the coral formations at the wall lip. The walls are steepest here, forming overhangs which cast their shadows on the slope Ⓓ.

105

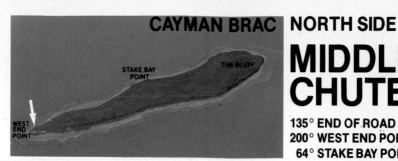

MIDDLE CHUTE

135° END OF ROAD
200° WEST END POINT
64° STAKE BAY POINT

DIVI TIARA
RESORT

106

Located about 500m (545 yards) east of the previous site and opposite the center of the landing strip. The site is sometimes divided in two (**Middle Chute/West Chute**) since there are several sand chutes gauged through the slope. The characteristic steep walls above the crack and the slope below are apparent here as well. The wall here is not as high, with the wall lip starting at a depth of 20-23m (60-66ft) and the wall itself (with the slope) at 30m (90ft).

Once underwater, the brilliant silvery white rivers of sand flowing down the slope contrast sharply with the dark and somber tones of the rock. A large chute is the most prominent attraction. The wide white chute becomes narrower as it gets deeper, and at a depth of 25m (75ft) becomes a real channel as it digs through the rock, while the walls get higher and higher and curve inwards nearly forming an arch **(A)**. Once past this point it again widens towards the base of the slope.

RUNWAY

135°

64° • 200°

N

(A)

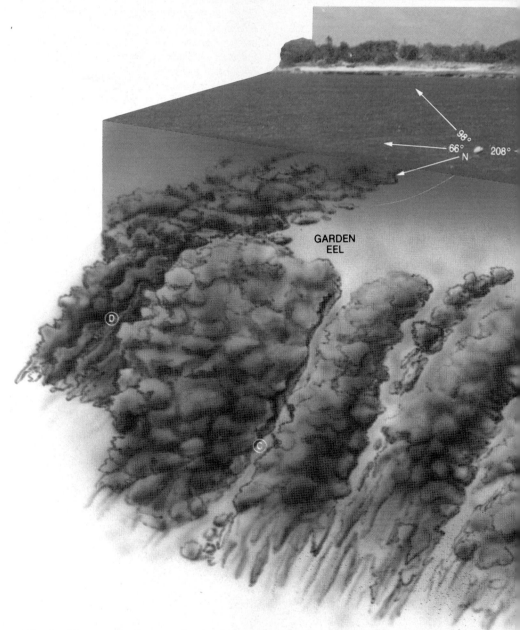

GARDEN EEL

The boat's remains lie at a depth of some 18m (55ft) on the flat sandy floor at the end of a long reef dotted with barrel sponges Ⓐ. Although this is a new wreck, it already has some permanent residents: a Green Moray and a Black Grouper are spotted with increasing frequency. There are usually quite a few Stingrays in the sandy area around the wreck also. Do not spend too much time here, for there is a lot more to see.

From the wreck continue along the western side of the elongated coral formation; the floor starts to slope downwards, the rocky walls loom up and suddenly a river of sand appears, plunging away into the depths Ⓑ. The walls on both sides of the chute curve inwards, forming a "gateway" to the sand river at a depth of 30m (90ft).

This is one of the most popular dive sites in the area, and justifiably so. A dive here is an underwater experience that combines wreck, sand chutes, canyons, shallow and wall dives in a single adventure. It is a relatively shallow site for the island, starting at 17m (50ft). The wreck is that of the 65ft Cayman Mariner which used to be a metal workboat and was operated by Cayman Energy Ltd. She was purchased by Brac Aquatic and deliberately sunk in 1986.

CAYMAN MARINER WRECK

EAST CHUTE

Continue east across the steep slope on your right, passing several narrow sand chutes that pour over the wall from the sand plain above. The third canyon is deeper and can even be considered a tunnel Ⓒ. Immediately afterwards a large pinnacle appears out of the blue depths and the slope turns into a

real wall. The head of the pinnacle is higher than the surrounding reef and forms a corner, which you follow along the wall Ⓓ. The wall face is home to many large gorgonians and sea-fans, and you could get lucky and run into the large Jewfish, the wall's permanent resident. Swim around the pinnacle and start your ascent along the slope behind it; this will bring you back to the sand plain and its colony of Garden Eels on the east side.

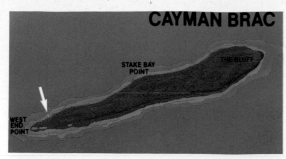

CAYMAN BRAC NORTH SIDE

CEMETERY WALL

66° STAKE BAY POINT
185° CONTROL TOWER
227° WEST END POINT

Named after the Cayman Brac cemetery which is almost in front of the site, this is a popular site. Several good relatively shallow second dive sites are nearby, the best of which is Grunt Valley. Cemetery Wall has the typical Cayman Brac topographic features; chutes, slope, walls and two interesting canyons.

The first thing you see is a wide sand chute which forks around a large coral formation Ⓐ at its end. The forks become narrower and narrower but remain navigable. Just remember that you are already at a depth of some 30m (90ft), and should turn around and investigate the other half of the site. You will cross two more canyons on the way back. The wall lip in this area is very steep and encrusted with barrel and tube sponges and sea whips Ⓑ.

The third canyon is the most interesting. It is very narrow, with the entrance more like an especially beautiful cave Ⓒ at a depth of 26m (80ft). The canyon twists and turns upwards, widening once it reaches the sand plain above.

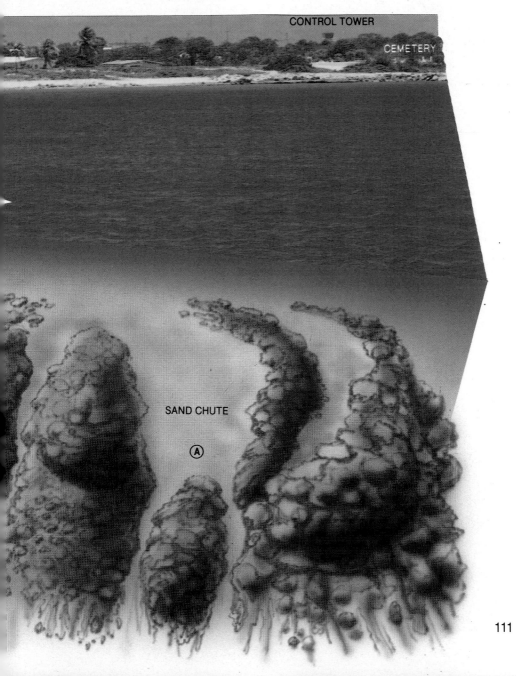

CONTROL TOWER

CEMETERY

SAND CHUTE

Ⓐ

111

GRUNT VALLEY

Located close to shore and to the east of the Cemetery Wall dive site, this is a vast area of shallow reefs that is superb as a second dive or for a long photography session. Grunt Valley is the best known among the various sites nearby, thanks to the extremely large schools of Grunts and Yellowtail Snappers that hang around the coral heads. These heads run perpendicular to the shore with a gentle slope from 7m (20ft) to 13m (40ft) and flat valleys between them. It is an outstanding place to hunt for macro photography prey such as invertebrates, nudibranches, coral fish arrowcrabs, file shells and shrimp.

Two typical Grunt Valley underwater seascapes

GREEN HOUSE

There are several shore areas in Cayman Brac that are especially suitable for snorkeling. One of these is located in a relatively isolated area opposite Stake Bay Point. The reef is fairly far off shore, and at first the sea floor is flat with a few small coral heads, but these quickly fill out, becoming a large area striped with long rows of coral lying perpendicular to the shore alternating with silvery white sand. Average depth is from 6-10m (15-35ft).

The tall coral heads are easily reached in a free dive

LITTLE CAYMAN

LITTLE CAYMAN

Little Cayman is the smallest of the three Cayman Islands, lying 126 km (79 miles) northeast of Grand Cayman. The waters around Little Cayman are considered by many the finest diving sites in the Caribbean. There are no restaurants, pubs, tennis courts or golf courses, only virginal nature, and diving, diving and more diving. If you plan to escape from civilization and spend your vacation exploring the fascinating depths, this is one of the few remaining isolated spots in the Caribbean that offers you a virtually unspoiled paradise to indulge yourself in.

Three independent dive operators are based on Little Cayman, and offer full facilities including equipment, accommodations, food, boats, etc. (See Dive Service Guidelines, page 188).

You can also dive Little Cayman from Cayman Brac. There are daily boat trips that provide a full day's diving, with an approximately 45 minute trip to Little Cayman, 3-4 dives and meals on board. Divers coming from Grand Cayman can choose the live-aboard boat that spends a week in Little Cayman.

The island is almost completely uninhabited (there are fewer than 20 permanent residents), there are only a few paved roads and the airport is a grass landing strip with no control tower. It is flat (the highest point of elevation not more than 13m (40ft) high) and densely covered with bush jungle and mangrove swamps which are populated by a multi-hued cacaphony of parrots, iguanas and birds.

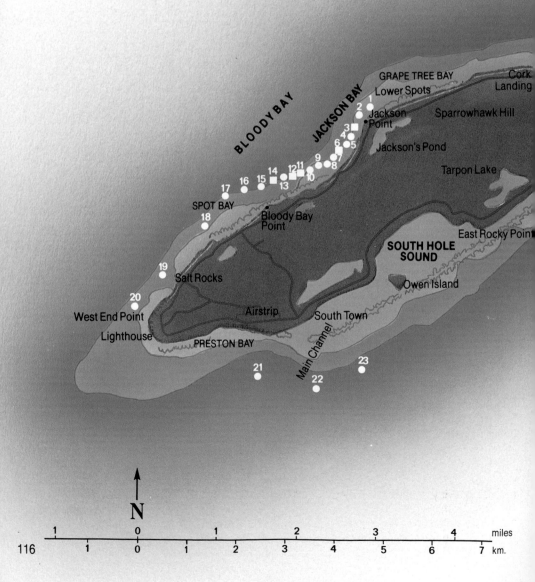

The most popular dive area is the famous Bloody Bay, so called after a legendary pirate battle in the misty past. Bloody Bay's major attraction is actually one long wall starting at Jackson Point extending westward to Spot Bay, some 4 unbroken km (2.5 miles) of diver's paradise. It offers everything a diver could ever want or dream of, starting at the relatively shallow depth of 8-10m (25-30ft). The upper part is rich in large coral heads on a clean, white, sandy floor and teems with abundant fish and marine life. The wall itself is a true wall (not a slope) and is punctured by hundreds of canyons, chimneys, caves and tunnels. In some places the wall ends in a step at a depth of 33-43m (100-130ft) sloping away afterwards, and in some places the wall simply disappears into the deep.

All the Bloody Bay dive sites are marked with buoys, but the sites themselves often have several names with sometimes confusing results. Frequently sites bear local as well as official names, while several sites sometimes have the same name. There are about 15 official sites along the Bloody Bay coastline, five of which are described in this book. In general, the names appearing in this book are the official ones as they appear on the official buoy bearing lists, although some of the more popular sites appear under other names.

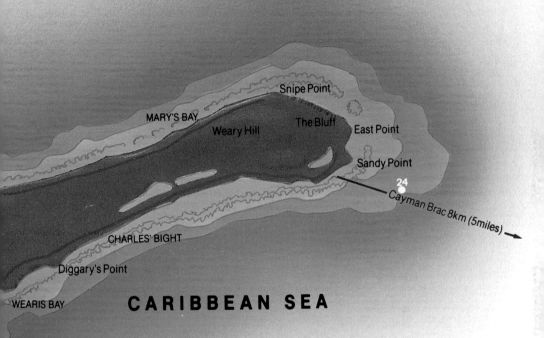

LITTLE CAYMAN DIVE SITES

NANCY'S CUP OF TEA
MAGIC ROUNDABOUT

WEST OF JACKSON POINT

Two narrow canyons (A) lead from the sand plain on the top of the wall and join together at the edge. There is a huge pinnacle jutting out from the top of the wall. The coral formation is separate from the wall and you can swim completely around it. This is the part called the **Magic Roundabout** (B). It is balanced on two other large coral formations that also jut out from the wall. The formations are separated by extremely deep canyons, but there is no problem entering them and photographing them from inside looking out C. This is a good place to take photographs of divers against a background of deep blue water at the canyon entrance.

Another special feature of this site is the height of the coral heads. The wall actually starts at a depth of only 13 m (40 ft), and the coral formation on which the pinnacle rests is at a depth of 22m (66ft). The base of the wall is at a depth of 33m (100ft), after which there is a step-like formation followed by a sandy slope covered with rocks that slopes sharply downwards and disappears into the

depths.

Also known as the **MAGIC ROUNDABOUT**, this is a group of large coral heads clinging to the wall lip like a jumble of giant warts, giving the site an unusual appearance not at all like the normal wall structure. The thickly encrusted site is located some 300m (327 yards) from Jackson Point or the third buoy from the corner.

There is rich variety of marine life, fish, soft coral, colorful sponges and deep water fish, with the occasional shark putting in an appearance in the lower depths. The canyons are very deep and it is a good idea to take a flashlight to light up the insides of the caves even if you are diving during the day. Finish the dive near the sand plain where there is also a lot to see, mainly near the coral heads.

119

JACKSON BAY

THE MEADOWS & EAGLE RAY ROUNDUP

WEST OF JACKSON POINT

The sandy sea floor, clean and white, is at a depth of 10m (30ft) in the center and 13m (40ft) near the wall lip which projects slightly. The coral heads in the middle Ⓐ reach a height of 5-7m (15-20ft) underwater. On the shore side there is an interesting mini wall rich in marine life Ⓑ which is at a depth of only 3m (10ft) so that non-divers can enjoy snorkeling in this area.

The sea floor slopes downwards at the wall lip. The crevices and tunnels lead away from the sand plain through the lip and spill out over the edge. There is a long coral formation on the western side that continues towards the wall, punctuated by a number of tunnels

120

The diagram represents the west side of Jackson Point. The Meadows and Eagle Ray Roundup are located below the western and central buoys which can be seen clearly in the aerial photograph. They are considered separate sites, but, as you can see from the photograph, are actually part of the same area where you can spend an entire day enjoying several types of dives, including a comfortable mixture of wall and shallow diving. The wall is punctuated by many large crevices and tunnels with dropoffs to about 30m (100ft). On a clear day diving at the sand plain above is like going for a swim in a giant aquarium.

and canyons which lead to an area whose character is slightly different Ⓒ. The coral heads are straighter and sharper here and look like small towers.

Northwest of the buoy is a clean, tubelike cave that is especially interesting. Enter from the side of the wall 🄳 and exit underneath the coral heads 🄴 directly opposite the mooring line.

Aside from the usual reef fish, you will most probably see Stingrays with their Jack escorts as well as large Parrotfish which burrow in the sand. There are Garden Eels on the west side and Eagle Rays in the open water, as well as the ubiquitous schools of Yellow Tail Snappers and Jacks.

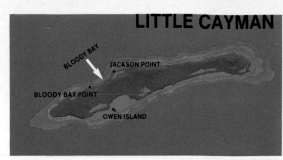

MIXING BOWL

THREE FATHOM WALL

84° EAST END OF SANDY BEACH
240° BLOODY BAY POINT

The wall itself is very steep and full of narrow canyons and coral. The wall lip lies at only 6.5m (20ft), a unique characteristic of the entire area, enabling snorkelers to enjoy a look at the enormous wall which disappears into the depths.

The sand plain is flat with many soft corals and yellow tube sponges growing between the coral heads. A Yellow Coney keeps watch on the mooring line, begging to be photographed (you can find him in the Fish Index, page 141). Above the sand plain are schools of Yellowtail Snapper, Horse-eye Jacks and a pair of Barracudas — one so old that its body has curved like a banana.

The wall ends suddenly in a deep sand chute (A) which pours over the sand plain onto the wall base at a depth of some 36m (110ft).

On the other side of the chute is the Mixing Bowl, which looks exactly as its name implies. There is an amazing variety of deep canyons, arches and caves all jumbled up together in one small area. Immediately after the chute is a narrow, deep canyon with a sandy bottom that starts at a depth of 33m (100ft). The lower part of the canyon is nearly completely closed, forming a pretty coral arch (B). The large coral heads in the central formation are separated by crisscrossing deep grooves above which looms a large, flat coral head (C).

There is a cave at the bottom that leads to the second canyon (D), which is also deep

and narrow and leads up to the sand plain. This is the large reef fishes' favorite spot; large Tiger Groupers and especially friendly Nassau Groupers can often be spotted. Coral abounds, including yellow and orange tubes, red cup sponges, orange elephant ear sponges and red finger sponges as well as plenty of gorgonians and sea-fans.

Trumpet sponge on the wall

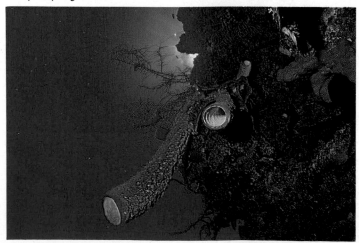

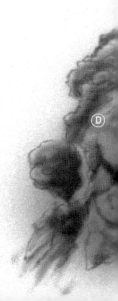

THREE FATHOM WALL is located very near the shore, right in the middle of **Bloody Bay** and marked by two buoys. These are very close together and are exactly opposite two triangular rocky projections jutting into the waterline. The entire area is sometimes treated as a single dive site while others divide it into two, since an underwater swim from one end to the other can take as long as ten minutes. For greater detail, the diagram of the site is laid out in two parts. This page covers the eastern dive site, the Mixing Bowl, while the western part of the wall is described on the next page.

OWEN ISLAND→

SOUTH HOLE SOUND

84° 240°

N

THE CAYMAN AGGRESSOR

ⓒ

Ⓑ

SAND CHUTE

Ⓐ

THREE FATHOM WALL

MARILYN'S CUT→

LITTLE CAYMAN BLOODY BAY

BLOODY BAY

JACKSON POINT

BLOODY BAY POINT

OWEN ISLAND

MARILYN'S CUT

HOLE IN THE WALL

84° EAST END OF SANDY BEACH
237° BLOODY BAY POINT

SOUTH HOLE SOUND

THE CAYMAN AGGRESSOR

84° 237°

N

D

THREE FATHOM WALL

← MIXING BOWL

The formations on the western side of **THREE FATHOM WALL** are completely different. The wall and lip are smoother, the coral formations smaller and less dense, with a giant pinnacle surrounded by deep canyons and an especially beautiful cave in the heart of the wall. The site lies under the western buoy some 116m (127 yards) from the first buoy.

Once underwater, face the lip wall and you will immediately make out the mushroom shaped pinnacle Ⓐ. The water under the boat is only 6.5m (20ft) deep, but there is a slope and the lip wall lies at a depth of 10m (30ft). This slope leads to a large, deep canyon that separates the pinnacle from the wall. There is another canyon on the other side so that you can swim completely around the pinnacle. The canyons are so cleanly etched that they look man made. The pinnacle base is narrower than its upper part and there is a squarish step Ⓑ going down to the base at a depth of 26m (80ft).

The eastern canyon is very deep and the floor widens the further in you go. Another canyon which looks like a cave and has openings in its roof branches off it Ⓒ and is parallel to the outside wall. The sea floor is flat and sandy as the cave widens and curves towards the back.

The entire area is an excellent spot for photographs with a wide angle lens, especially when there is a diver in the cave and his air bubbles waft out through the openings in the roof Ⓓ and past the walls of the cave and canyons which are covered with red and yellow tube sponges.

From here, you can continue east to the **Mixing Bowl**, but remember that you have a 116m (127 yards) swim.

If the boat has moved from the first buoy to the one above you, the Barracudas and other fish will be awaiting you there. You may also find Parrot fish and Triggers and it is a good place to photograph a Queen Triggerfish.

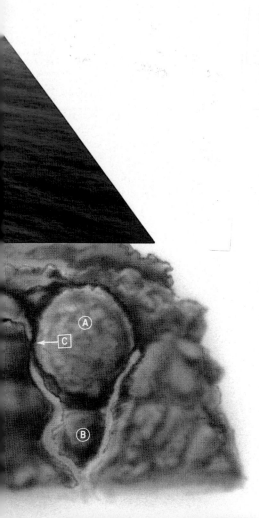

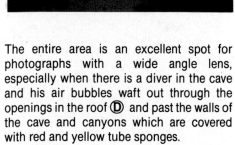

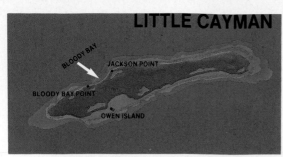

LITTLE CAYMAN   BLOODY BAY

THE
CHIMNEYS
RANDY'S GAZEBO
58° JACKSON POINT
222° BLOODY BAY POINT

126

Also known as **RANDY'S GAZEBO**. The site is similar to **THREE FATHOM WALL** with its steep, smooth wall that provides interesting diving on both sides, but here the wall is shorter and can be visited in a single dive. The Chimneys are located some 400m (438 yards) east of Bloody Bay Point and the site is easy to spot since the beach opposite is rocky, not sandy, with a triangular projection jutting into the water **(A)**. Plan two dives here, a deep dive first along the length of the wall and a second shallow dive to take in the area above the wall and the sand plain which is also very interesting.

The mooring line is attached to a chain fastened to the mouth of the cave or big chimney **(B)**. West of the buoy line there is a narrow canyon that suddenly becomes a deep, steep (90°) canyon. It is very wide at its upper end and you will find the entrance to the vertical chimney **(C)** near the pinnacle. The exit is at the base of the canyon at a depth of some 26m (80ft). From here you can swim across the base of the wall **(D)** to the east side, where there is a deep canyon and a coral arch **(E)** on which flourish sea feathers, basket sponges, yellow tube sponges and others. The coral seem to be part of a cave separate from the pinnacle. After exploring this area, you can return to the sand plain through the canyon near the arch **(F)** or start a diagonal ascent towards the step that runs along the entire length of the upper part of the wall **(G)**. This step is actually a deep crevice at the top of the wall, and at its center is the entrance to the large cave to which the buoy chain is attached **(B)**, leading to the buoy line and a hot cup of coffee in your boat moored patiently above.

FISH INDEX

Given the overall misuse and general destruction of our waterways, Cayman waters are among the clearest and least polluted in the world, providing the finest conditions possible for the development of flora and fauna. The islands have no rivers to deposit sediment onto the crystal clear beaches, and constant streams of water bring plankton to the area to complete an unbroken circle of life. The fringing reefs, canyons, slopes and bottomless depths enable larger fish to reach the shore, while at the same time provide protection for more vulnerable life forms. There is an impressive variety of species, ranging from the smallest reef dwellers to open water giants.

This index is intended to present those marine species most commonly encountered by the diver. Most entries are coral dwellers living in or near the reef habitat. These fish are famous for their flamboyant coloring and well developed camouflage as well as for the impressive anatomical adaptations allowing them to feed comfortably in and around the reefs. The larger open water species have developed hydrodynamic shapes enabling them to move rapidly through the water.

Important: Whenever diving in tropical waters do not touch or play with any species that remains passive and does not flee at your approach. A mobile marine animal with this characteristic has some kind of natural defense, be it a mild or deadly poison, unusual color or taste. Don't take your chances — the result could be unpleasant.

Hawksbill Turtle   *Eretmochelys imbricata*

Although the turtle is not a fish, it deserves an honorable mention in this section. The famous Cayman turtle farm has done much to preserve the turtle population, in spite of the fact that it is a commercial enterprise. Each year the farm releases thousands of young turtles into the sea. The Caymans are the only place on earth where a diver meets up with turtles with such amazing regularity and has the opportunity to photograph them. No wonder the turtle has been adopted as the symbol of the Cayman Islands.

RAYS

Every dive in the Caymans brings you face to face with an extraordinary variety of fish species that make their home in its seas. But few of these evoke the drama and excitement of an encounter with the rays that are so common in these waters. These unusual and elegant creatures present a challenge to diver and photographer alike-the challenge of achieving familiarity with the unfamiliar.

Rays belong to the class *Chondrichthyes* (cartilaginous fish), and are members of its largest order, *Rajiformes*, which numbers 16 families and about 340 species including skates, guitarfish and sawfish. We have chosen to focus on rays belonging to the *Dasyatidae* family which possess a number of distinctive features. First and foremost, they share the fact that their fins have fused together to form disks, with eyes and spiracles on the upper side and mouth on the lower side well positioned to eat off the sea floor. Their skeleton is made of cartilage and they lack scales altogether.

Five of the most common Caymanian rays are the **Manta** and the **Eagle Ray,** whose pointed wings are specially adapted to transport these strikingly graceful fish through their open water habitat, and the disk-like **Southern Stingray, Yellow Ray** and **Electric Ray** which are sand-dwellers.

The giant **Manta** might not be an everyday sight in the Caymans, but it is one you are unlikely to forget. Mantas have a worldwide distribution in tropical to warm temperate waters. The **Devil Ray** (*Mobula hypostoma*) and the **Atlantic Manta** (*Manta birostris*) are the two mantas most commonly encountered in the Caribbean. The Devil Ray is the smaller of the two, 1.2m (4ft) in length. It is sometimes seen in groups of four to six moving close to the surface, or along the edge of the reef. This manta is renowned for its spectacular leaps out of the water. The origin of its name is fairly obvious. In common with all mantas, it displays two flexible protrusions called cephalic fins that form narrow lobes protruding like horns on either side of the head. These appendages are used chiefly to facilitate the entry of small pelagic food organisms into the manta's wide mouth.

The Atlantic Manta has an impressive wing-span of 6m (18ft). It delights in hovering elegantly with the tips of its wings just breaking the waterline. It is easily identified thanks to its unmistakable size.

The **Spotted Eagle Ray** (*Aetobatus narinari*) closely rivals the manta in its beauty and grace. The Eagle is very common in the Caymans, and is most frequently encountered along the North Wall. Although it prefers open water, it sometimes penetrates shallow lagoons (see **Eagle Ray Pass**, page 50). The Eagle Ray is characterized by its jutting triangular head. Its eyes and spiracles are located on either side of its head rather than on top of it like other rays. It has wings spanning 1.8m (5.5ft) supremely adapted to "flying" through the water, quite unlike the disk-like build of its relatives which prefer to creep along the sandy ocean floor. Its back is adorned with white spots on a gray-blue background. Its tail is long and whip-like, and is armed with one or more stings.

The third ray of the group, the **Southern Stingray** (*Dasyatis americana*) is by far the most famous and most popular of all the Caymans' rays, and is responsible for one of the Islands' best-known attractions: **Stingray City** (see page 42). Its body, shaped in the form of a rhomboid disk, is characteristic of sand-dwellers, and it does indeed spend most of its time in the sandy patches between coral heads, sometimes even digging itself into the sand. Its protruding eyes and spiracles are located on the upper surface of the head. Its tail is broad at the base tapering off towards the end where its poisonous sting is situated, with a type of fin running halfway down its length. Its coloring varies between gray and dark brown or even black, but the region of the throat is light-hued. In the Caymans, tame stingrays enliven their diet of sand-dwelling organisms with fish and other food eaten straight out of divers' hands.

The **Yellow Stingray** (*Urolophus jamaicensis*) is elliptical in shape. Its tail, with its poisonous sting, is shorter than its body. The total length of this ray seldom exceeds 40cm (16 in). Its body coloring ranges between light and dark brown, with a profusion of yellowish blotches. It seeks out sand plains covered with turtle grass, and may sometimes be seen squatting under rocks.

The **Lesser Electric Ray** (*Narcine brasiliensis*) is somewhat similar to the Yellow Stingray in appearance, but very different in character. Also known as the Torpedo Ray, this sand-dweller has two electric organs on either side of its body capable of stunning its prey. Its round disk-like body is covered with brown marks arranged symmetrically on a dark yellow background. It has a length of only 30cm (12 in).

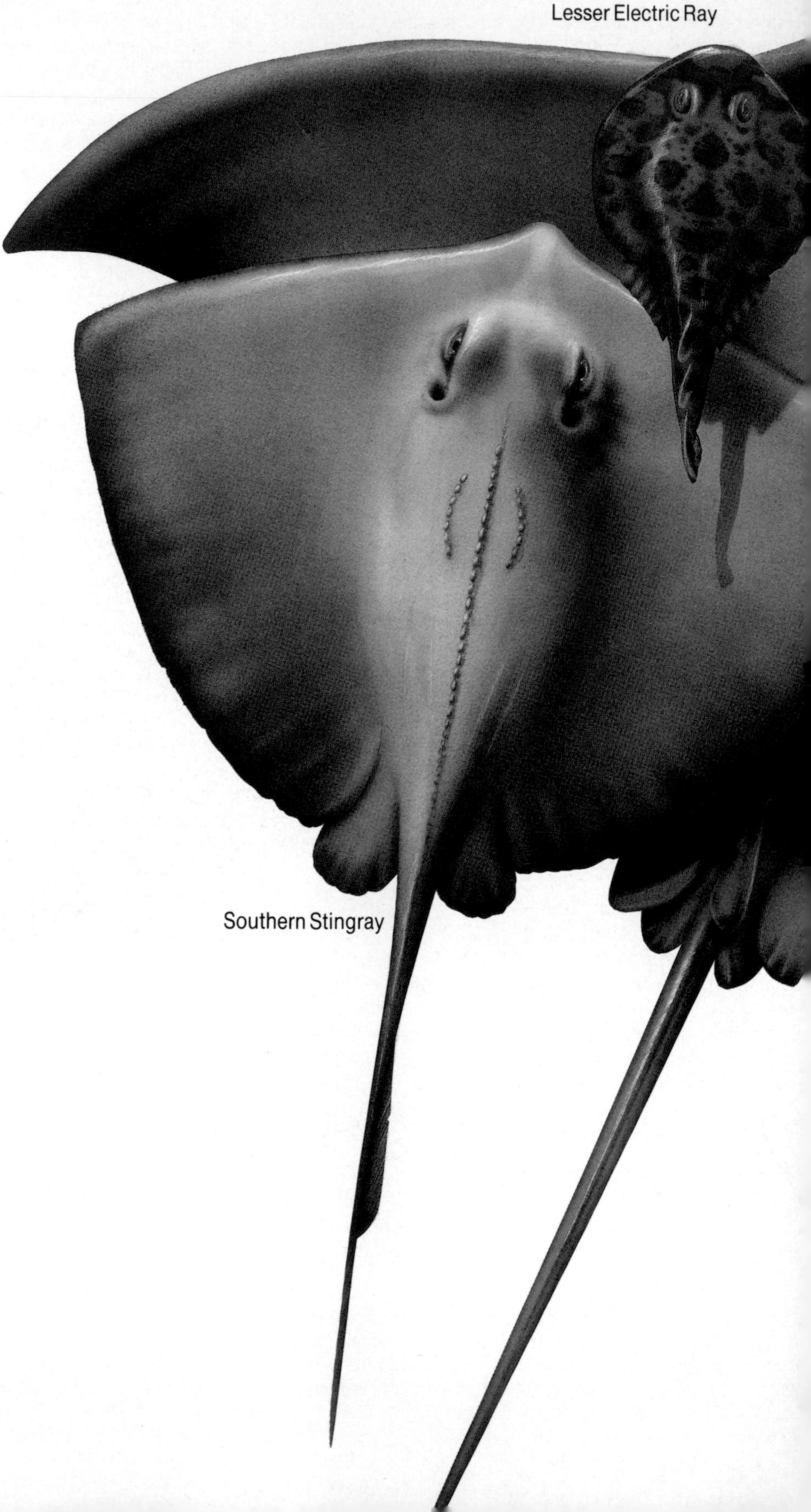

Lesser Electric Ray

Southern Stingray

Atlantic Manta

Spotted Eagle Ray

Yellow Stingray

TARPONS

There is little doubt that the **Tarpon** has come to symbolize diving in the Caymans. A number of sites are named after this fish, which is also a permanent guest in many others. A large fish which may reach a length of 2.7m (8ft), the Tarpon is characterized by its vivid silver color. It looks almost as if it has been wrought in burnished stainless steel. The lower jaw juts forward, while the diagonal mouth points upwards. The Tarpon is a highly prized game fish which puts up a fierce struggle when hooked and leaps out of the water to great heights.

Tarpons are generally found in sandy-bottomed canyons at fixed locations where they move about in smallish schools, although you may sometimes come across an isolated individual elsewhere. They are easily approached and photographed. Diving into a canyon among a school of Tarpon which seem to hover motionless around you, is a thrilling experience typical of diving in the Caymans.

The accompanying photograph was shot at the famous **Tarpon Alley**—where else?!

Tarpon   *Megalops atlanticus*

MORAY EELS

Moray Eels are among the most respected citizens of the tropical reef community. These snake-like nocturnal predators can develop to impressive, even frightening, dimensions. Yet they are misanthropic hermits which prefer a policy of peaceful retreat to close encounters with divers—unless, of course, a diver's hand searching for lobster in the wrong hole triggers off an attack of claustrophobia.

Green Moray are the mightiest of their clan in the Caribbean region, often growing to 1.8m (6ft) or more—just like the one in this picture, photographed in the region of the **Oro Verde**, see page 87.

Green Moray   *Gymnothorax funebris*

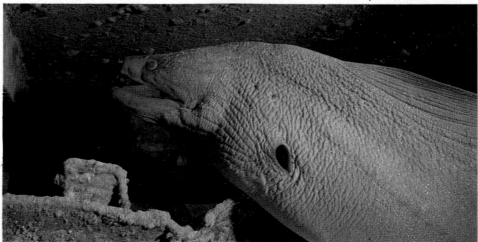

Spotted Moray are one of the more populous species found among the Islands. They average about 60cm (2ft) when fully grown, and are thus considerably smaller than their green cousins. They are easily identified by the many spots which are the source of their common name.

The **Goldentail Moray** is smaller than its two relatives, and seldom exceeds 60cm (2ft) in length. Like the Spotted Moray, it displays a profusion of dots set on the yellowish background which characterizes it, and is thus a particularly colorful photographic target. Its common name is derived from the more dominant yellow tones of its tail.

Goldentail Moray   *Muraena miliaris*

GARDEN EELS

Although each eel digs its own individual tunnel-abode, **Garden Eels** are found in communities which sometimes number hundreds of members. The Garden Eel never leaves its home. Its tail is permanently fixed in its tunnel, while the rest of its body moves freely outside, swaying gently in the current with the head pointed upstream to collect plankton. When danger threatens, the whole community sinks silently backwards into their tunnels, their heads disappearing last.

Garden Eels are found exclusively on flat, sandy ocean floors at depths of 6-27m (20-80ft). Their bodies are snake-like, elongated and very narrow (1cm in diameter, and up to 60cm in length). You need lots of patience in order to photograph these creatures. Approach them cautiously, crawling rather than descending on them from above, and photograph while lying flat on the seabed. Or simply lie in wait for them, and film them as they re-emerge from their tunnels. (See the chapters on the **East Schute** and the **Oro Verde** sites for more information).

Garden Eel *Gorgasia sillneri*

GLASSEYE SNAPPER

This reddish fish with large, glassy eyes is nocturnal, and is seldom seen during the daylight hours. But on days when the sky is heavily overcast, you might have the good fortune to spot an occasional one just outside its lair. The reddish tone of this snapper can rapidly turn to silver (as is evident in the accompanying photograph) when irritated by the flash of your underwater electronic gear.

Glasseye Snapper *Priacanthus cruentatus*

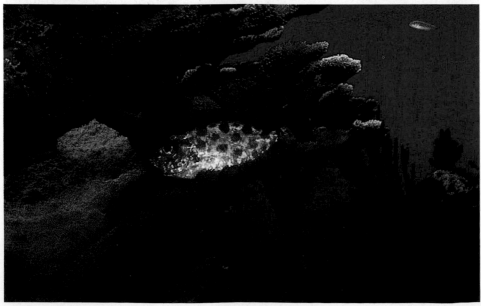

TRUMPETFISH

With a remarkable and distinctly amusing anatomy, the ubiquitous **Trumpetfish** found on almost every coral formation in these waters provide an excellent target for your camera. Whether immobile, drifting, or even standing on their heads (see photograph), their excellent plastic camouflage offers versatile protection. They will often assume the headstand position when in the vicinity of bush-like coral, in order to maximize the effectiveness of their camouflage. Smaller fish and shrimps are the primary prey of these efficient hunters. Don't be misled by their slow and lazy manner—they can fin at such blurring speed that their victims just seem to vanish into their bell-shaped mouths. They prosper in the waters of the Caribbean, often reaching a length of about a meter (3ft) at full growth.

Trumpetfish   *Aulostomus maculatus*

SQUIRRELFISH

The majority of **Squirrelfish** belonging to the genus *Holocentrus* are reddish in color and have the large eyes so characteristic of nocturnal feeders. The most common member of the clan, *Hobcentrus rufus*, photographed overleaf, has clear cut markings, with red and white body stripes and a diagonal white bar below the eye.

The **Blackbar Soldierfish** is easily identified by virtue of the dark bar running diagonally behind its eyes. Needless to say, this is the source of its common name.

Blackbar Soldierfish *Myripristis jacobus*

SEA BASS

Encompassing some 400 species, this family is familiar to every diver. The majority of its members are bottom dwellers found on the sandy sea floor, or in caves and holes. Most of them are carnivorous, and are easily recognized thanks to their large mouths. Although sea bass can range in length from a few centimeters to almost 4m (12ft), the larger specimens found in the Caymans reach about 2.7m (8ft) and weigh in at 300kg (700lbs).

GROUPERS

Groupers belong to the far-flung sea bass family. **Nassau Groupers** are among the most populous species found in Caribbean waters. Look for the dark bands on the body of this fish, the dark spots around its eyes and the black saddle on the caudal peduncle. Its bands are typically brown or olive in color, with pale green, gray or even white in between. This unusually friendly fish, which easily reaches over a meter in length (3-4ft), quickly learns to feed from a diver's hand.

Nassau Grouper *Epinephelus striatus*

Diagonal tiger bars give the **Tiger Grouper** its name. Unlike other groupers, Tigers are not bottom feeders, and are well worth the effort of trolling just near the surface. They grow to more than half a meter (30in) in length.

Tiger Grouper *Mycteroperca tigris*

JEWFISH

The adult **Jewfish,** the largest sea bass of them all, can easily be identified by its huge size alone. A mature member of this species can measure 2.7m (8ft) and carry 300kg (700lbs). Jewfish are usually found under wrecks, beneath ledges or in large caves.

Jewfish   *Epinephelus itajara*

CONEY

Coney are quickly identified by their sharp split-color pattern. The body is usually covered with blue spots, and its upper part, seen from eye level, is very dark brown to greenish or red. For even more positive identification, look out for the two black spots on the tip of the lower jaw.

Coney   *Cephalopholis fulva*

SAND PERCH
Consistent with their common name, **Sand Perch** live in holes or under rocks on the ocean floor where divers often find them resting. They are easy to recognize thanks to their banded body pattern and the perennial blue lines on their heads. Some specimens reach a length of 30cm (1ft).

Sand Perch   *Diplectrum formosum*

HARLEQUIN BASS

Harlequin Bass are immediately set apart from others of their kind thanks to a very distinctive color pattern. They show dark markings ranging from brown to black, with white above and a yellowish coloring below. The Harlequin Bass has a length of about 10cm (4in) at maturity.

Harlequin Bass   *Serranus tigrinus*

INDIGO HAMLET

The **Indigo Hamlet** is also easy to identify with its dark-blue body and contrasting light-blue bars. It is not too common in the Cayman region.

Indigo Hamlet   *Hypoplectrus indigo*

FAIRY BASSLET

Despite its diminutive size of 7.5cm (3in), this fish is a real eye-catcher! Its front half is deep purple and its back half vivid gold, while a distinctive black patch is clearly visible on its dorsal fin. It hovers above the reef and may sometimes be seen to swim upside-down beneath the corals. To photograph it, you'll need a macro lens and lots of patience!

Fairy Basslet   *Gramma loreto*

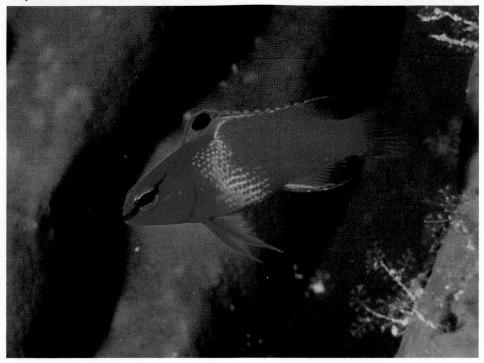

JACKS

Bar Jacks are the most common members of the *Caranx* family sighted in this region. They are often seen in large schools near the reefs. Look for the dark bar covering most of the lower part of the tail, then extending forward to the base of the dorsal fin. About 30cm (1ft), when fully grown.

Bar Jack   *Caranx ruber*

Yellow Jacks are unmistakable with their pale yellow-green and silver coloring, and yellow fins and tail. They average about a meter (3ft) in length at adulthood.

Yellow Jack *Caranx bartholomaei*

Horse-eye Jacks, a very common family, are generally open water dwellers where they move in schools of various sizes. Unlike the Yellow Jack, only the tail of this fish is yellow while the rest of its body is silver. It enjoys close encounters with divers, and at certain locations, schools of Horse-eyes will congregate right below your boat!

The **Black Jack** is a very rare fish which is, nevertheless, easily identified thanks to its very dark tail and fins. It usually travels alone or in pairs rather than in schools, and prefers open water habitats.

Black Jack *Caranx lugubris*

The **Greater Amberjack** has a well-defined amber band running from eye to tail set against a dark body and a silver-white belly.

Greater Amberjack *Seriola dumerili*

SNAPPERS

Snappers can generally be recognized by their distinctive profile. Their heads have a long triangular shape, whose upper margin slopes more sharply than the lower. Most members of this family dwell inshore near the ocean bottom.

A common specimen sure to be recognized is the **Gray Snapper**, which sometimes exhibits a wide and dark oblique stripe running from the tip of its snout across the eye and fading out in the direction of the dorsal fin. Some Gray Snappers survive to grow to a meter (3 ft) in length.

Gray Snapper   *Lutjanus griseus*

The name **Yellowtail Snapper** is a bit misleading because the broad yellow stripe characteristic of this fish begins at the snout and extends to the tail. But identification is easy if you remember to look for a rose-toned lower body and yellow fins. Yellowtail are a common reef species, and live in the shallow draft directly above the coral formations.

Yellowtail Snapper   *Ocyurus chrysurus*

Mutton Snapper   *Lutjanus analis*

DURMS (CROOKERS)

Durms are family set apart by their long flag-like dorsal fins and by the distinctive durmming sounds they make.

Highhat have dark brown or black stripes set against a silvery white background. They are about 22cm (9in) long when fully grown.

Spotted Drum also reach 22cm (9in) and may easily be identified thanks to their white-spotted back and tail regions. The juvenile Spotted Drum is almost identical to the juvenile **Jackknife:** both share an extremely elongated dorsal fin and a wide black bar running from the top of the fin to the tip of the tail. The juvenile Drum, however, is distinguished by the black spot on its snout.

Spotted Durm   *Equetus punctatus*

Highhat   *Equetus acuminatus*   Spotted Drum juv.   *Equetus punctatus*

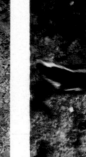

BERMUDA CHUB

This sea chub, often seen in Caymans, rapidly darkens when cutting under coral and rock. It is about a half-meter (18in) at full size.

Bermuda Chub   *Kyphosus sectatrix*

French Grunt   *Haemulon flavolineatum*   Smallmouth Grunt   *Haemulon chrysargyreum*

GRUNTS

Commonly named because of their tendency to grunt when removed from the water, this family is closely related to the snapper. Finning in huge schools above the reefs during the day, they scatter at night to feed on the ocean bottom. The **French Grunt** is probably the most familiar specimen. It is pictured here with the **Smallmouth Grunt**. Note how Smallmouth Grunts have few prominent and parallel yellow stripes, while those on the French Grunt are more abundant and not parallel.

The photograph alongside shows a school of **Bluestriped Grunt** accompanied by a solitary **White Grunt**. A Bluestripe can mature to a size of almost a half-meter (18in). Look for its silvery body and yellow stripes. White Grunts have blue heads with yellow stripes, a dusky spot on their tails, and often display a dusky region on their sides, too.

148

Bluestriped Grunt *Haemulon sciurus*   White Grunt *Haemulon plumieri*

Sometimes you will notice a vividly colored fish in amongst schools of grunt. This distinctive individual, the **Spanish Grunt,** has clear black stripes along the length of its body and an extremely noticeable yellow stripe on its back. Its fins are black with narrow yellow margins. Unlike the other grunts, the Spanish Grunt prefers to keep to itself or to congregate in small groups.

Spanish Grunt   *Haemulon macrostomun*

The 30cm (1ft) long **Porkfish** is also a member of the grunt family. It is easily recognized thanks to two black bars on the head, combined with yellow and silvery-white lines on the body.

Porkfish   *Anisotremus virginicus*

GOATFISH

Goatfish are easily identified by their two prominent whiskers used for searching out small invertebrates in the sand. **Yellow Goatfish** are often seen finning in the company of grunts in large schools on the reef. They are most likely to be found in spurs and grooves systems. Note the yellow stripe from the eye to the base of the tail. Yellow Goatfish have a length of up to 30cm (1ft) when mature.

Yellow Goatfish   *Mulloidichthys martinicus*

BUTTERFLYFISH

Butterflyfish and Angelfish are close relatives. Both are found in tropical waters around the globe, and constitute some of the most colorful elements in the reef kaleidoscope. Adults live in pairs, while the young are usually solitary. **Spotfin Butterflyfish** are swiftly distinguished thanks to the black mark on the tip of their dorsal fin, hence their common name. This long dusky mark may pale when exposed to light.

Spotfin Butterflyfish *Chaetodon ocellatus*   Foureye Butterflyfish *Chaetodon capistratus*

The **Foureye Butterflyfish** maintains the largest population in the Caribbean family. A round black eye-spot on the body gives it its name. **Banded Butterflyfish**, with their black and white bars, seem to be a deliberately composed work of art. The patterns displayed by butterflyfish are evolutionary adaptations designed to confuse their enemies: the bars and false eye-spots make it difficult for predators to chart the direction of their course.

Banded Butterflyfish   *Chaetodon striatus*

ANGELFISH

Angelfish are immensely curious and wholly without fear, often posing within a few feet of your lens. **Queen Angelfish** bear the most intricate and beautiful patterns in the entire family, and were so named for the crown-like electric-blue spots on their foreheads. **Gray** and **French Angelfish** are similar to the Queen, but are less colorful. The **Rock Beauty** is just that, with a dark body set off by a yellow head and tail.

Queen Angelfish   *Holacanthus ciliaris*

Rock Beauty   *Holacanthus tricolor*

French Angelfish   *Pomacanthus paru*

Gray Angelfish   *Pomacanthus arcuatus*

DAMSELFISH

Damselfish are a large family of small, very colorful fish. A few species live in beds of sea grass or on the rocky ocean bottom, but the majority are reef residents. These territorial fish guard their turf diligently, and doubly so when they have eggs to protect.

The **Bicolor Damselfish** gets its name, naturally enough, from its split-color pattern: dark in front and pale behind. It has a maximum length of about 9.5cm (4in).

Threespot Damselfish have a yellowish body. They reach 9-12cm (4.5in) in length. When assigning titles to your slide collection, you are advised to note the black spots on their dorsal fins together with a black saddle at the base of their tails.

Beaugregory is a memorable name for a striking demsel maturing to about 17cm (7in). You won't forget its yellowish body topped with bluish stripes and dots on the head, together with a large dark-blue spot on the dorsal fin.

The **Sergeant Major** is one of the most common damselfish found throughout the Caribbean. Five black bars set against yellow ones on the upper side and a silver-gray background give it its name. It is 17cm (7in) long when fully grown.

Bicolor Damselfish *Eupomacentrus partitus*

Threespot Damselfish *Eupomacentrus planifrons*

Beaugregory *Eupomacentrus leucostictus*

Seargeant Major *Abudefduf saxatilis*

Brown Chromis are usually olive-brown above and silver-gray below. Note the little white saddle behind the dorsal fin. They are seen in large schools which feed in open water above the reef. The Brown Chromis stops growing at about 12-15cm (5-6in).

Brown Chromis   *Chromis multilneata*

The overall bright blue of the **Blue Chromis** is edged with a remarkable pair of dark black-green stripes reaching from its head to the tip of its tail. These 12cm (5in) specimens live and feed above open and patch reef.

Blue Chromis   *Chromis cyanea*

WRASSE

One of the most populous families of reef dwellers, wrasse represent a marvelous spectrum of anatomical forms and are found in sizes varying from a mere 2.5cm (1in) long to the enormous dimensions of the Napoleon Wrasse *(Cheilinus undulatus)* of the Indo-Pacific.

Hogfish   *Lachnoldimus maximus*
Spanish Hogfish , Bluehead Wrasse   *Bodianus rufus, Thalassoma bifasciatum*

The spectacular **Hogfish** reach 60cm (2ft) and are common in the waters off Cayman. They possess a unique ability to alter color depending on whether they are moving or at rest. Hogfish are readily identified by three long dorsal spines. **Spanish Hogfish** distinguish themselves by their strong vivid colors. The upper two-thirds of their bodies are bluish violet or plum colored, the remainder is bright yellow.

Bluehead Wrasse represent an excellent example of sex-related color change in a single species. This photograph shows a school of yellow- phase Bluehead feeding on lobster. They may be juveniles or adults of either sex. However, some of the males and females develop into terminal-phase supermales bearing the distinctive color pattern you can see on the supermale in the bottom left-hand corner of this picture. Whether ordinary or super, they can grow to a length of 15cm (6in).

Bluehead Wrasse   *Thalassoma bifasciatum*

SPADEFISH

The **Atlantic Spadefish** is immediately perceptible as it makes its appearance in the reef habitat, often swimming in small groups. Its name is derived from its anatomy which bears a striking resemblance to the suit of Spades in a pack of cards. It is easily identified thanks to its extended dorsal and anal fins, and its dark vertical bars. It generally reaches half a meter (18-20in) in size, although very occasionally a large individual may grow to be as much as a meter (3ft) in length.

Atlantic Spadefish   *Chaetodipterus faber*

GLASSY SWEEPER

The **Glassy Sweeper** is so named because immature members of this family are virtually transparent. It is sometimes also called the **Copper Sweeper** thanks to the copper-toned body coloring displayed by adults. This is a tiny fish, only 10-11cm (5in) long. It spends most of the day in the gloom of caves, and ventures forth mainly after dark.

Glassy Sweeper   *Pempheris schomburgki*

PARROTFISH

The common name "parrotfish" originates in the combination of bright colors and beak-like jaws displayed by this family. Regardless of genus or species, members of this clan are unusually energetic and active, and move without cease throughout the day. Divers find them just about everywhere along the reefs, migrating constantly from coral to coral while breaking off and crushing their required quota of polyps. You can observe and listen to these rock crushers in coral seas around the globe. Seeing as they are in constant motion, you need to have an element of luck and surprise on your side in order to get good photographs of them. Parrotfish stop only at nightfall when they search out a safe resting place in crevices, grottoes or caves until dawn. The generic common name encompasses an immense multitude of species which are difficult to distinguish and catalogue accurately. There is considerable disagreement, even among marine biologists, as to the allocation of correct scientific names.

Blue Parrotfish — *Scarus coeruleus*

Queen Parrotfish — *Scarus vetula*

Stoplight Parrotfish   *Sparisoma viride*

GREAT BARRACUDA

Rarely more than 1.5m (5ft) long, but occasionally considerably larger, **Great Barracuda** are found in deep and shallow waters throughout the Caymans. Stories describing attacks by large barracuda are quite common in popular literature. Nevertheless, most hard evidence indicates that they do not attack divers. Just remember not to annoy these magnificent creatures. And don't forget to carry your catch tied to a line—not to your weight belt. Barracuda do, after all, hunt fish.

Black dots on the sides of the Great Barracuda easily distinguish it from its relatives. Adults are silver to steel-gray in color with about twenty dusky bars on the upper side. Incidentally, you are advised to remember that very mature barracuda may sometimes be poisonous.

Great Barracuda   *Sphyraena barracuda*

FLOUNDERS

Flounders are one of the most interesting of the reef-dwelling families, and go to prove that fact is often stranger than fiction! Many people tend to think that, like the stingray, the flounder's eyes are located on its back. This is not actually the case. This fish, which seems to float permanently on its belly, is actually positioned on its side.

When the flounder is born it resembles any other fish. But after a few days, one of the flounder's eyes migrates to the other side of the fish, and assumes its characteristic position. Flounders are distinguished by the fact that the right eye migrates to the left side, hence the name "lefteye flounders." With soles, on the other hand, the left eye migrates to the right side.

Flounders are masters of camouflage. They tend to float on the sandy bottom where their flat body and coloring make it almost impossible to spot them. They sometimes bury themselves in the sand, with only their eyes exposed, on the lookout for unsuspecting prey. They may also change their body color according to the environment in which they find themselves. In the accompanying photograph, taken at Parrot Reef, you can just make out a **Peacock Flounder**—if you're persistent enough, that is. It may be identified by means of the blue rings which adorn its body, and by its long dorsal fin which is erect during periods of rest.

160 rest.

Peacock Flounder   *Bothus lunatus*

SCORPIONFISH

Contrary to the popular mythology about sharks, the **Scorpionfish** is one of the most dangerous reef residents for divers. Stingers on its upper dorsal fins, containing a strong poison, spring forth automatically under pressure. The unwary diver need only touch or step on them to activate their possibly fatal defensive action. This passive predator neither attacks nor approaches the explorer. The great danger it poses stems from its behavioral and physiological adaptations. It tends to lie motionless on the reef or sea floor waiting for an unsuspecting fish to swim past, while its stone-like appearance enables it to maintain perfect camouflage with its environment. The Scorpionfish is characterized by three dark bars on its tail.

Scorpionfish   *Scorpaena plumieri*

Special note: Unless you have done your zoological and botanical homework thoroughly, a basic rule to follow in tropical waters is to avoid touching the flora and fauna of the reef and to remember to wear good tennis shoes or fins, obviously ones without holes! Should you have the misfortune to be stung, consult a doctor immediately.

SURGEONFISH

Surgeonfish are commonly named for the two sharp spines, like a surgeon's scalpel, found at the base of the tail—an easily identified feature. These are excellent weapons, so be careful not to be slashed by a sweeping tail.

Bluetang Surgeonfish catch the eye with their deep-blue coloring contrasted by clear yellow scalpels. The youngsters are lemon-yellow, but evolve to the characteristic intense blue as they mature at 30cm (1ft). The **Ocean Surgeon** is altogether brown to gray, apart from a lighter pale bar at the base of its tail. The margins of the tail and the fins are blue.

Bluetang Surgeonfish   *Acanthurus coeruleus*

Ocean Surgeonfish   *Acanthurus bahianus*

TRIGGERFISH & FILEFISH

The name "triggerfish" derives from a locking mechanism located in the dorsal fin. When the forward dorsal spine is erect, the second spine moves forward and locks it into an upright position. There is no way to release the lock and push it down without releasing the second spine. This trigger spine operates like a hook, making it difficult, if not downright impossible, to pull a triggerfish from a wedged defensive position in the corals.

Queen Triggerfish are among the most beautiful fish in the Caribbean. Although very versatile and adept at color change, two stripes of bright blue remain constant below the eye no matter what the camouflage adopted.

Queen Triggerfish   *Balistes vetula*

The **Black Durgon's** overall dark coloring makes it stand out in the reef habitat. These fish display two white stripes at the base of their dorsal and anal fins. Two blue stripes extend like horns around the eye in the direction of the forehead.

Black Durgon   *Melichthys niger*

163

Scrawled Filefish are set apart from other species of a like appearance by their distinctive markings. An olive or a brownish body contrasts with lines and spots in bright blue, while most of the caudal fin is dusky or black. But note that they can alter their coloring to match their surroundings. Sometimes they are seen drifting along at odd angles, nose down, propelled solely by their dorsal fin. Most individuals measure an average of a meter (3ft) at maturity.

Scrawled Filefish   *Alutera scripta*

Scrawled Filefish   *Alutera scripta*

Whitespotted Filefish may easily be identified by means of the white spots which cover their body—hence their common name. Although they are generally golden brown with a dark tail, Whitespotted Filefish can rapidly change their general background color.

Whitespotted Filefish   *Cantherhines macrocerus*

Whitespotted Filefish   *Cantherhines macrocerus*

165

TRUNKFISH

A fascinating, photogenic, but rather shy species which exhibit scales that have evolved to form a curious system of linked armored plating with holes for the eyes, mouth and fins. They make good hunting with your camera, not only because of the delight they inspire on a slide screen, but also because their slow, languid motion makes them easy to frame in the lens.

Scrawled Cowfish seem to be the most numerous in these waters and are quickly catalogued in your photographic notebook thanks to the two horns on the top of their heads. They reach about 50cm (20in) at maturity.

With an average length of about 13cm (5in), the **Smooth Trunkfish** is the tiniest member of the clan. Note that they discharge a toxic substance which may kill other fish in an aquarium or in the bait tank.

Scrawled Cowfish   *Acanthostracion quadricornis*

Smooth Trunkfish   *Lactophrys triqueter*

166

PUFFERS

Puffers have evolved the remarkable adaptation of being able to make themselves into unswallowable morsels by inflating themselves with water, just like balloons.

Bandtail Puffers are easily distinguished by the row of round, dark spots stretching from the chin to the base of the caudal fin, for which they are named. They are found throughout Caribbean waters. Divers may confirm identification by noting the yellowish tone on the upper half of the body.

One of the most familiar puffers found in the Cayman region is the **Sharpnose** which inhabits a wide variety of habitats. Look for a color range stretching from brownish-orange to dark brown on the upper part of the body, with tiny blue spots on the head as well as a miniscule size of only 10-13cm (4-5in) in adulthood.

Bandtail Puffer   *Sphoeroides spengleri*

Sharpnose Puffer   *Canthigaster rostrata*

BALLOONFISH

Seen fully inflated in this photograph, the **Balloonfish** protects itself by erecting a series of strong, sharp spines from head to tail in addition to inflating its body like a puffer. When deflated, the spines fold back against the body. The largest of the Caribbean family shows a basic color ranging from pale brown to greenish tones set against a white belly.

Balloonfish   *Diodon holocanthus*

PORCUPINEFISH

This fish is the largest member of the Spiny Puffer family and has been known to reach a length of 60cm (2ft). It displays a basic color toning from pale brown to greenish, contrasted by a white belly. Small dark spots cover the entire body, the fins and tail. The Porcupinefish is a solitary feeder living off sea urchins, crabs and molllusks, all of which it crushes with its strong, incisor-like jaws. Although it is a reef dweller, it may sometimes be found in grassy areas and near mangroves.

Porcupinefish   *Diodon hystrix*

SNOOK

The **Snook** is an extremely tasty game fish favorite among fishermen. This long, silvery fish is easily identified through the prominent dark lateral line extending along the length of its body. Its forehead is depressed giving its extended snout an angular appearance. This fish lives in small schools numbering only a few members and frequents shallow areas near mangroves. In season sometimes, an individual Snook will be encountered in the reef area, lying in wait in caves and on ledges for its prey of herrings or silversides. It has a body length of between 30-120cm (1-4ft).

Snook   *Centropomus undecimalis*

SILVERSIDES

Silversides are an extremely populous family of cave dwelling fish. In season, you will encounter them on practically every dive massing as a vast, living silver cloud which engulfs and thrills you. Various individual species like Silversides may be identified, but on the whole silversides are chiefly remarkable for the stunning collective impression they make. These fish are the primary prey of Tarpons (see page 134) and Snook.

Silverside

U/W PHOTOGRAPHY

MARTIN SUTTON

UNDERWATER PHOTOGRAPHY

Twenty or thirty years ago dive magazines were full of articles and pictures on young trim spearfishermen proudly displaying their latest trophy. How times have changed! Today's dive journals are packed with colorful shots of healthy reefs, rainbow-hued fish, divers interacting with the underwater world, man in harmony with nature.

The transition has paralleled the dynamic growth of Scuba diving and the rapid development of high quality, easy to use camera and video systems. Underwater photography is no longer the domain of the handyman able to construct clumsy but watertight cases for his land camera or the well-heeled with the resources to bankroll a Hasselblad or Rolleimarine underwater housing. Today, with just a little practise, anyone can shoot great pictures using compact systems that are a breeze to operate.

Nowhere is this change in perception more in evidence than in the Cayman Islands which boast the widest selection of photographic possiblities and services available to the travelling diver. In this chapter we explore some of the photographic opportunities Cayman affords, and provide a listing of professionals who can assist you along your way.

Let's imagine a diver planning a trip to Cayman, who knows a little about underwater photography and has a basic camera set-up. How should he prepare for the trip? What should he expect to find on the island? What can he hope to return home with?

BEFORE THE TRIP

Before the trip, the system should be checked. Make sure that the O-rings are in good shape by removing them and pulling them gently through finger and thumb, feeling for cuts or nicks. Check battery power and see that the camera fires the strobe when triggered. It's a good idea to assemble the system completely to ensure that all parts that are supposed to be there are, in fact, there. O-rings, batteries and camera spare parts are available on the island, but prices will tend to be some 25% higher than you are used to paying due to extra shipping and import duty. To save disappointment, check before you leave home.

You may wish to bring film with you as it is fairly expensive on the island. If so choose a relatively slow film such as an ASA 100 or ASA 125 for greater color saturation and fine grain. The waters around the island are unusually crystal clear and fast films are unnecessary.

WHAT TO EXPECT

When planning what equipment to bring, remember that our waters offer unlimited possibilities for all types of photography. Wall dives are perfect for the drama of wide angle. Panoramic vistas with colorful sponges and gorgonians in the foreground and a pinpoint of sunlight in the corner of the frame are easily composed in the bright, clear water. Shallow dives provide wonderful static subjects such as yellow sponges and vivid purple sea-fans, along with a vast array of tame fish willing to pose for just a small handout.

Perhaps the most exciting dive in the Cayman Islands is Stingray City. To capture the action best use a wide angle lens with either a strobe or a URPro color correcting filter. Resist the temptation to chase the rays — they can all swim faster than you, and tail shots won't win any prizes!

Night dives are the perfect studio for macro systems. Moving at a slower pace, the diver encounters myriad small critters easily captured in the frame of an extension tube. With its fixed settings, the macro system is easy to use in the dark.

WHAT TO BRING

The simple answer is BRING EVERYTHING! All types of photography are not only possible in Cayman, but are also easy. The water is clear, subjects abundant and unafraid, and dive sites easily accessible. Pack your wide angle equipment, your macro gear, your close-up attachments and your standard lenses as you will use them all! If you lack some of these, don't despair, several operations on the island offer complete equipment rental. The rates are affordable and renting offers the added advantage of a quick photo lesson before you step out of the store. The same stores will be able to process your film quickly and often the knowledgeable staff are willing to give quick critiques that will help with your subsequent shooting.

If your interest is particularly photographic, you may want to choose a dive operation that caters to photographers: setting up their boats with the photographer in mind, diving small groups, choosing sites well suited to photography and staffing their boats with photo instructors.

Should the worst happen and a piece of photo equipment breaks or floods, you could hardly be in a better place than Cayman. At least three stores are set up to offer camera and strobe repair, some even going so far as to offer a loaner unit while yours is being fixed.

PHOTO CLASSES

No matter what stage of development you are at as a photographer, a photo class is likely to be beneficial. The neophyte can often obtain great shots and an in-depth understanding in only a few days and the more advanced shutterbug will improve with discussion of composition or the special effects of multiple lighting. For the non-photo buddy, perhaps a modelling class would be just the ticket, allowing a greater involvement with the photographer's interest, and a greater understanding of what he is trying to achieve. Whatever level of instruction you seek, Cayman has it. Cayman is home to some of the world's best known and most respected photo instructors. In some cases, classes are scheduled on certain dates, in others, classes can be set up around your schedule. Whichever you choose, the chances are that a class will dramatically improve your shots and justify every penny spent.

UNDERWATER VIDEO

If the development of underwater photography has been rapid, then the development of underwater video has been meteoric. Until the mid 80's, underwater video did not really exist. Since that time, the genre has grown at an incredible pace and now threatens to become more popular than underwater photography. Perhaps it is the ease with which anyone can shoot underwater video, or the immediate gratification of plugging into any TV set to watch the results. Or perhaps it is the fact that with video there is movement, which to many is the beauty of diving in the first place. A picture of a ray can be exciting, but for many, does not rival the thrill of seeing the ray glide effortlessly in the shallow waters of the North Sound of Grand Cayman. Underwater video IS easy but the constant evolution of video formats often renders obsolete systems that may still be relatively new. For that reason, and because of the fairly high cost of video housings, many people are reticent to get into this format. Cayman offers them an alternative. A number of stores rent underwater video systems at inexpensive rates. In some cases rental includes editing and the inclusion of titles and a soundtrack to complete the production. For those who just want to try video, or are unwilling to invest in a system, renting provides an economical way to get into underwater video.

WHY BOTHER

We have all been on dive boats and have seen the well equipped underwater photographer crawling out to the boat laden down like a pack mule. We have all wondered at the expense and the apparently unfathomable dials and controls, buzzers and lights. Why do they bother? Is it really worth it? Ask any photographer and you will receive essentially the same reply and the same motivation.. having tried unsuccessfully to describe the underwater world they take to photography to explain more eloquently a magnificent phenomenon that few will ever see. Pictures take the place of words, video takes the place of imagination, offering in colorful images a glimpse into a world that man has not yet despoiled. In truth, photography may be even more than that. It is a state of understanding, one of being attuned with and a part of a magnificent world that only a handful are privileged to know. And, significantly, it enables the representation of that world however poorly, to our fellow man. No matter on what level our mind operates, photography will recharge tired batteries, enrich the soul and bring back fond memories of happy times. Photography is for everyone and nowhere is it better than in the Cayman Islands.

PHOTO FACILITIES AVAILABLE IN CAYMAN

The Cayman Islands have a number of operations that can help you with your photo needs. Some specialize in photography and video while others offer photo services in addition to their other services. Here is a rundown on services available on the Islands at the time of writing.

FISHEYE OF GRAND CAYMAN — Grand Cayman
Fisheye is the most specialized photo-dive operation on the island of Grand Cayman. It offers three customized boats, all crewed by photo and video instructors. Fisheye conducts daily dives to the West Wall, the North Wall and Stingray City, and to the South Wall on weekends. Full photo and video rentals are available as is daily film processing. Fisheye has been teaching a wide range of photo, video and underwater modelling classes longer than anyone else on the island. Chief photo instructor is Martin J. Sutton, who has taught underwater photography for over fifteen years, both in Cayman and in the Red Sea.
Fisheye is located at Trafalgar Place, on West Bay Road, one mile north of the Holiday Inn. Tel: (809)-94-74209 Fax: 1-(809)-94-74208

UNDERSEA PHOTO AND DIVE SUPPLY — Grand Cayman
Undersea Photo and Dive Supply, located in the Falls Shopping Center, just north of the Holiday Inn is a retail store that offers photo and film sales, camera and video rentals and a wide selection of books on photography. Tel: 1-(809)-94-74686

SUNSET HOUSE — Grand Cayman
Sunset House was one of the island's first dive hotels. Located south of George Town, the island's capital, Sunset House is the home of The Cathy Church School of Underwater Photography. The Cathy Church School offers a variety of photo classes from beginner to expert levels as well as photo and video rental, daily film processing and Nikonos camera repair. Tel: 1-(809)-94-97111

TIARA BEACH HOTEL — Cayman Brac
Photo Tiara at the Tiara Beach Resort on Cayman Brac offers a wide range of services including photo classes, daily film processing and photo and video rental. Photo pros at Photo Tiara are the well known Chris and Donna McLaughlin. Camera repair is also available. Tel: 1-(809)-94-87553

BRAC PHOTOGRAPHICS — Cayman Brac
Brac Photographics is Ed Beaty's operation located at the Brac Reef Beach Resort. Ed offers photo rental, photo instruction, film processing and individual video shoots. Tel: 1-(809)-94-87340

Yellowhead Jawfish

CAYMAN'S UNDERWATER PHOTOGRAPHERS

The Cayman Islands provide unparalleled opportunities for underwater photography, and attract scores of photographers, both amateurs and professionals. yearly. In the following pages, we are proud to host the following internationally acclaimed professionals who live and work in the Caymans: Courtney Platt, Chris & Donna McLaughlin, Anne Davis & Wayne Hasson, Cathy Church and Martin Sutton.

COURTNEY PLATT

P.O. Box 62 Savannah, Grand Cayman, B.W.I.
Phone: (809)-94-71671

Courtney Platt is a professional underwater photographer who began as a hobbyist in 1976. Based in Grand Cayman since 1983, his collection of local marine life images has become one of the most extensive. Decorative art prints and commercial assignments are his mainstay. Because of a deep-seated interest in marine life, Courtney goes to extraordinary efforts to capture aesthetic representations on film. As a result, his photography has won numerous awards and international recognition. In addition to his underwater photography,

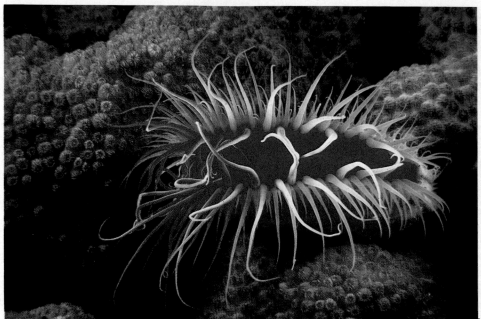

The Flaming Scallop, or File Shell (lifesize).

A Green Sea Turtle takes a peek at the tree-line on Seven Mile Beach.

he made over a thousand dives as pilot of RSL's deep diving submersibles in Grand Cayman. His "Deep Wall" photography appeared in the November 1988 *National Geographic Magazine* article, "Down the Cayman Wall." His photographs have also been in *Time, Forbes, Skin Diver, Scuba Times, The Cayman Year Book,* etc. For custom color prints or assignments call: (809)-94-71671 or write to P.O. Box 62 Savannah, Grand Cayman, B.W.I.

A rare Fingerprint Shell (4X lifesize).

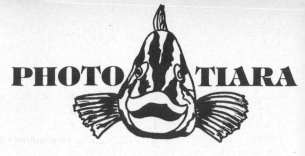

CHRIS & DONNA McLAUGHLIN
Photo Tiara
P.O. Box 238 Stake Bay
Cayman Brac, B.W.I.

Chris and **Donna McLaughlin** are the resident photo pros for **Photo Tiara.**

Photo Tiara is the full service photography department of the Divi Tiara Beach Resort. Camera/video rentals, video shoots, daily film processing, photographic supplies and a complete range of instruction are featured in conjunction with the dive program of Dive Tiara.Personalized instruction and state-of-the-art equipment are available year round, and the beautiful walls and reefs of Cayman Brac and Little Cayman are your studio. Photo Tiara's quality instructional program in conjunction with Dive Tiara and the Divi Tiara Beach Resort has caused Nikon to select Cayman Brac as a destination for their Nikon School of Underwater Photography and Nikonos Shootout.

Chris and Donna began teaching underwater photography professionally in 1981 in Bonaire at the Flamingo Beach Resort. They are experienced photographers and videographers whose work has appeared in *Skin Diver, National Geographic World, Sports Illustrated, Fortune,* and numerous other magazines, newspapers and the book *Bonaire.* Video clips of their work have been on nationwide television programs such as *Good Morning America* and *Hour Magazine.* Today, in addition to teaching underwater photography, Chris and Donna take photographs for weekly slide presentations, brochures, stock sales and for the fun of it.

ANNE DAVIS and WAYNE HASSON
Aggressors International Ltd
P.O.Box 1882, Grand Cayman, B.W.I.
Phone: (809)-949-5551, Fax: (809)-949-8729

Anne Davis and **Wayne Hasson**, Managing Directors of the Aggressor Fleet, have over eight years of experience diving and photographing in the Cayman waters.

While working as a team, Anne has modelled and appeared in such publications as *National Geographic, Skin Diver, Ocean Realm, Scuba Times* and many others.

Wayne, a well published underwater photographer, has been featured in these magazines as well as travel related publications. As the founder of the "Cayman Islands Petting Zoo," Wayne spent many years working and photographing with the famous Waldo, the 6ft moray, Snaggletooth, Bugsy and their friends.

Most of their time is spent hosting trips aboard the Aggressor Fleet state-of-the-art live-aboard dive boats and teaching Nikon Technical Seminars.

CATHY CHURCH
Sunset Underwater Photo Centre and Gallery

P.O. Box 479 Grand Cayman, B.W.I.
Phone: (809)-949-7415 FAX: 809-949-7101

For over sixteen years, **Cathy Church** has been photo editor of *Skin Diver Magazine,* and co-author of five books and over two hundred articles on underwater photography. In 1988 she started the **Sunset Underwater Photo Centre and Gallery** as a base for her broad photographic activities, which include working on her latest book *Creative Underwater Photography.* Her photo centre combines her talents with those of several others, including Mike Mesgleski and Herb Rafael, providing the skills to do everything from teaching a beginner which end is the front of the camera, to handling the toughest ad jobs.

Herb photographed this squid during one of his photo courses with Cathy. She liked it so much that she decided to marry him. (Photo by Herb Rafael/Cathy Church Photography).

During photo courses Cathy enjoys working underwater with her students. Even beginners can enjoy professional results similar to this photo taken by Mike. (Photo by Mike Mesgleski/Cathy Church Photography).

Cathy's favorite type of photographs are
those that work both light and shadows;
photos that, like all good art, change as you
look at them for a long time.
(Photo by Cathy Church).

MARTIN J. SUTTON
Fisheye Photo Services
P.O.Box 30076, Seven Mile Beach,
Grand Cayman, B.W.I
Phone: (809)-947-4209, Fax:(809)-947-4208

Martin J. Sutton, founder and co-owner of Fisheye Photo Services is one of Cayman's longest established underwater photographers and photo instructors. With a long list of credits in both still photography and video, his work has been seen in magazines in the US, Europe and Middle East and on such TV networks as NBC, CNN and the Discovery Channel.

Teaching a variety of classes in all aspects of underwater photography with lectures and slide presentations developed over ten years of courses, Martin has taught more students about this fascinating hobby than any other instructor on the island.

Before arriving in Cayman, Martin spent five years diving the Red Sea, and each year leads small groups back to this and other underwater wonderlands.

DIVE SERVICE GUIDELINES

The following information has been gleaned from the diving clubs themselves and various other sources. Naturally, a book has a longer life than a magazine or advertising brochure and the offering and facilities can change quickly. Therefore, some of the information may not be relevant after a period of time. We recommend using this guide as a general source of information which will give you an idea of the type and variety of activities and facilities available on Cayman.

FISHEYE PHOTOGRAPHIC

Owner/Manager:	Martin Sutton, Ed Uditis.
Address:	P.O. Box 30076, Seven Mile Beach, Grand Cayman.
Telephone:	(809)-947-4209.
Fax:	(809)-94-74208.
No. of Tanks:	90.
Dive Boats - No:	3.
Length & Capacity:	1x26 ft (14 divers); 1x23 ft (6 divers) 1x24 ft (6 divers).
Daily Trips:	2 tank morning dive; 1 and 2 tank afternoon dives.
Night Dives:	Tuesdays and Thursdays.
Special Dives:	Yes.
Courses:	Daily photo courses/video courses.
Photo Processing:	Yes.
Photo Rental:	Yes.
Video Rental:	Yes.
Accommodation:	Can be arranged at Anchorage View condominiums.
Dive Shop:	On Trafalgar Sq., West Bay Rd.

DON FOSTER'S DIVE CAYMAN LTD.

Owner/Manager:	Mervyn Cumber.
Address:	P.O. Box 151, George Town Grand Cayman.
Telephone:	(809)-947-5132, 1-800-83-DIVER.
Fax:	(809)-947-5133.
No. Of Tanks:	300.
Dive Boats - No:	7.
Length & Capacity:	1x36 ft (14 divers); 2x52 ft (20 divers); 1x54 ft (20 divers); 2x60 ft (25 divers); 1x28 ft (8 divers).
Daily Trips:	2 tank morning dive; 1 tank afternoon dive & snorkel trips.
Night Dives:	Mondays and Thursdays.
Special Dives:	Stingray City daily - North Wall
Resort Courses:	Full certification and specialty courses available and resort courses daily.
Accommodation:	The Radisson Resort Hotel Packages with other 7 Mile Beach Hotels & Condominiums.
Photo Processing:	Yes (6E).
Photo Rental:	Yes, plus instruction.
Video Rental:	Yes, plus custom video.
Dive Shop:	Radisson Hotel & Royal Palm Beach.
Special Comments:	Don Foster's Dive also offers sub-see explorer underwater viewing boat, watersports center , Emerald Eyes Catamaran sunset cruise & private charters.

BRAC AQUATICS LTD.

Owner/Manager:	Denise & Winston McDermot.
Address:	P.O. Box 89, West End, Cayman Brac.
Telephone:	(809)-948-7429.
No. of Tanks:	350 AL-50, 63/80 SUPE 80
Dive Boats - No.:	4.
Length & Capacity:	Reefrunner 50ft; Bogue Runner 32ft; Brac Runner 45ft; Little Cayman Diver 65ft.
Daily Trips:	Yes.
Night Dives:	Yes.
Special Dives:	Deep diving specialty.
Resort Courses:	Open Water (1)/(2).
Courses:	Yes.
Photo Processing:	Yes.
Photo Rental:	Yes.
Video Rental:	Yes.
Dive Shop:	At Brac Reef Beach Resort, South Side, Cayman Brac, Tel: (809)-948-7429.

PARROTS LANDING WATERSPORTS PARK

Owner/Manager:	Gregory Merren.
Address:	P.O. Box 1995, South Church Street, Grand Cayman.
Telephone:	(809) 949-7884, 949-7769.
Fax:	(809) 949-0294.
No. of Tanks:	132.
Dive Boats - No.:	2.
Length & Capacity:	1x28 ft (8 divers); 1x 32 ft (16 divers).
Daily Trips:	2 Tank dives depart daily at 8a.m. and 1p.m. 1 tank dives depart daily at 1p.m. Stingray City trips depart daily at 9a.m. and 1p.m.
Night Dives:	Shore night dives nightly, boat night dives on request.
Special Dives:	On request.
Resort Courses:	Resort courses and full certification courses taught daily.
Courses:	PADI and NAUI courses, Basic Scuba to Asst. Instructor Certification.
Photo Processing:	No.
Photo Rental:	Yes.
Video Rental:	Yes.
Accommodation:	In conjunction with local hotels and condominiums.
Dive Shop:	Retail and rentals. Located on South Church Street, half a mile from George Town.
Special Comments:	PARROTS LANDING features a park, boat dock, and excellent shore diving 5 sites adjacent to facility including Devil's Grotto.

TREASURE ISLAND DIVERS

Owner/Manager:	Ashton Ebanks
Address:	P.O. Box 1817, Grand Cayman.
Telephone:	(809) 949-4456.
Fax:	(809) 949-7125.
No. of Tanks:	280.
Dive Boats - No.:	3.
Length & Capacity:	3x45 ft (30 divers).
Daily Trips:	2 Tank morning dives (wall & reef dive); 1 tank afternoon dives.
Night Dives:	Twice weekly.
Special Dives:	Trips to Stingray City 3 times weekly.
Resort Courses:	7 days a week.
Courses:	Open Water Certification; Open Water Completion, Advanced Open Water Specialties.
Photo Processing:	On site.
Photo Rental:	On site.
Video Rental:	On site.
Accommodation:	TREASURE ISLAND RESORT (290 rooms & condominiums).
Dive Shop:	Located on beach, approximately 100 yards from resort.

SOUTHERN CROSS CLUB

Owner/Manager:	Donna Emmanuel.
Address:	South Hole Sound, Little Cayman, Cayman Islands.
Telephone:	(809)-948-3255.
No. of Tanks:	60.
Dive Boats - No:	2.
Length & Capacity:	1x27 ft (12 divers); 1x18 ft (4 divers).
Daily Trips:	2 tank morning dive; 1 tank afternoon dive.
Night Dive:	On request.
Special Dives:	Bloody Bay Wall.
Accommodation:	On site.
Dive Shop:	On site.

RON KIPP'S BOB SOTO'S DIVING LTD.

Owner/Manager:	Ronald L. Kipp
Address:	P.O. Box 1801, Grand Cayman.
Telephone:	(809) 949-2022.
Fax:	(809) 949-8731.
No. of Tanks:	400.
Dive Boats - No.:	8.
Length & Capacity:	16-54 ft (4-20 divers).
Daily Trips:	2 Tank dives, 1 tank dives, North Wall, South Wall and Stingray City trips offered daily.
Night Dives:	Tuesdays and Saturdays, Wall Night Dive on Thursdays.
Special Dives:	North Wall, South Wall, Stingray City, wall night dives.
Resort Courses:	Daily.
Courses:	Full Certification, Open Water Completion, Advanced Open Water.
Photo Processing:	Yes (E-6 and Print).
Photo Rental:	Yes.
Video Rental:	Yes.
Accommodation:	Holiday Inn and numerous condominium properties on Seven Mile Beach including Plantation Village, Beachcomber, Villas of the Galleon and London House.
Dive Shop:	Holiday Inn Dive Shop on Holiday Inn Beach; Soto's Coconut in the Coconut Place; SCUBA CENTER near the Lobster Pot Restaurant.

CAYMAN KAI RESORT

Owner/Manager:	Carson Ganci.
Address:	P.O. Box 1112 Northside, Grand Cayman.
Telephone:	(809)-947-9556.
No. of Tanks:	100.
Dive Boats - No:	2.
Length & Capacity:	1x20 ft (16 divers); 1x34 ft (18 divers).
Daily Trips:	2 tank morning dive; 1 tank afternoon dive.
Night Dives:	On request.
Special Dives:	On request.
Resort Courses:	Yes.
Photo Rental:	Yes.
Video Rental:	Yes.
Accommodation:	On site.
Dive Shop:	On site.

"QUABBIN DIVES" CAYMAN LTD.

Owner/Manager:	Arthle Evans.
Address:	P.O. Box 157, George Town, Grand Cayman.
Telephone:	(809) 949-5597.
Fax:	(809) 949-7117.
No. of Tanks:	Approx. 225.
Dive Boats - No.:	3.
Length & Capacity:	1x45ft V-hull "Quabbin D-too" (24 divers) 1x36ft V-hull "Quabbin Diver" (16 divers) 1x39ft V-hull (16 divers).
Daily Trips:	2 Tank morning dives depart at 8a.m. 1 tank afternoon dives depart at 1.30p.m. (minimum of 4 divers).
Night Dives:	Twice weekly as well as on demand, (minimum of 6 divers).
Special Dives:	1 Tank Stingray City dives; educational dives.
Resort Courses:	Afternoon pool sessions followed by morning boat dive.
Courses:	PADI and NAUI training facility, Resort to Asst. Instructor certification.
Accommodation:	35 Air-conditioned rooms with ceiling fans and kitchenettes. 30 Poolview. 4 Ocean front Swimming pool Jacuzzi, Ocean front Bar and Restaurant, three quarters of a mile from George Town.
Dive Shop:	Yes.

RED SAIL SPORTS

Owner/Manager:	Rod McDowall
Address:	P.O. Box 1588, George Town, Grand Cayman.
Telephone:	(809) 949-8745.
Fax:	(809) 949-8808.
No. of Tanks:	190x80 cu ft; 10x63 cu ft.
Dive Boats - No.:	2.
Length & Capacity:	2x45 ft (28 divers).
Daily Trips:	2 Tank morning dives (wall dive plus shallow reef or wreck dive); 1 tank afternoon dive (shallow reef or wreck).
Night Dives:	Tuesdays & Fridays.
Special Dives:	Saturday morning: North Wall & Stingray City.
Resort Courses:	Daily — pool lesson given twice each morning, diving on the afternoon dive boat.
Courses:	Open Water certification; Advanced through Divemaster Courses (PADI).
Photo Processing:	Not available on site (pickup at Hyatt Regency hotel).
Photo Rental:	35mm snapshot cameras.
Video Rental:	8mm or VHS video rental, or private video.
Accommodation:	Hyatt Regency, Grand Cayman.
Dive Shop:	Beach Shop — Seven Mile Beach (across from the Hyatt Regency, adjacent to Hemingways). Can also sign up for activities in the Sundry Store or at Senses Boutique at the Hyatt Regency.
Special Comments:	RED SAIL SPORTS also offers a full range of diving equipment rentals, as well as full watersport activities.

PETER HUGHES DIVE TIARA

Owner/Manager:	Divi Resorts, General Manager — David Feinberg.
Address:	P.O. Box 238, Stake Bay, Cayman Brac
Telephone:	(809)-948-7553.
Fax:	(809)-948-7316.
No. of Tanks:	250.
Dive Boats - No.:	6.
Length & Capacity:	1x40 ft (20 divers).
Daily Trips:	2 Tank morning boat dives, 1 tank afternoon boat dives.
Night Dives:	Yes.
Special Dives:	Little Cayman.
Resort Courses:	Yes.
Courses:	Yes.
Photo Processing:	Yes.
Photo Rental:	Yes.
Video Rental:	Yes.
Accommodation:	70 Air-conditioned apartments; superior, deluxe, luxury and 1 bedroom, several with television and whirlpool jacuzzi bath.
Dive Shop/s:	On site dive shop.
Special Comments:	We offer lighted tennis courts, watersports, snorkeling, fishing trips, and birdwatching.

AGRESSOR FLEET LTD.

Owner/Manager:	Wayne & Anne Hasson.
Address:	P.O.Drawer K, Morgan City, LA 70381 U.S.A.
Telephone:	(800)-348-2628.
No. of Tanks:	80.
Dive Boats - no.:	7.
Length & Capacity:	110 ft (18 divers).
Daily Trips:	No, week trip.
Night Dives:	Yes.
Special Dives:	North Wall Grand Cayman, Little Cayman.
Resort Courses:	Yes. Certification courses, Nikonos U/W Photography Seminar.
Photo Processing:	Yes.
Photo Rental:	Yes.
Video Rental:	Yes.

CAYMAN DIVING SCHOOL

Owner/Manager:	West Indies Properties
Address:	P.O. Box 1308, Grand Cayman.
Telephone:	(809) 949-4729.
No. of Tanks:	70.
Dive Boats - No.:	Not available.
Daily Trips:	Shore diving, specializing in instruction.
Night Dives:	By appointment.
Resort Courses:	Twice daily.
Courses:	Certification courses to all levels.
Accommodation:	By arrangement.
Dive Shop:	Located on the waterfront within ten minutes walk of George Town.

SAM McCOY'S DIVING LODGE

Owner/Manager:	Sam McCoy.
Address:	14 Rochambeau Ave. Ridgefield, CT 06877 U.S.A.
Telephone:	(203)-438-5663.
No. of Tanks:	36.
Dive Boats - No:	2.
Length & Capacity:	1x30 ft (8 divers); 1x20 ft (4 divers).
Daily Trips:	2 tank morning dive.
Night Dives:	On request.
Accommodation:	Yes.
Dive Shop:	Yes.

SUNSET HOUSE DIVERS

Owner/Manager:	Adrien Briggs
Address:	P.O. Box 479, George Town, Grand Cayman.
Telephone:	(809) 949-7111; (800-854-4767).
Fax:	(809) 949-7101.
No. of Tanks:	500.
Dive Boats - No.:	5.
Length & Capacity:	2x36 ft (18 divers); 1x32 ft (12 divers); 1x32 ft (16 divers); 1x45 ft (20 divers) High power CAT.
Daily Trips:	2 Tank morning dives, North Wall trips, morning and afternoon Stingray City trips
Night Dives:	Yes.
Special Dives:	Computer Manta Dives.
Resort Courses:	Yes.
Courses:	PADI, NAUI certification courses, upgrades.
Photo Processing:	Yes.
Photo Rental:	Yes.
Video Rental:	Yes.
Accommodation:	59 Air-conditioned rooms total, all with private bathrooms. Including 2 air-conditioned apartments All rooms have phones. Freshwater pool and Jacuzzi.
Dive Shop:	Located on property.

SUNSET UNDERWATER PHOTO CENTRE AND GALLERY

Owner/Manager:	Cathy Church
Address:	Sunset House P.O. Box 479, George Town, Grand Cayman.
Telephone:	(809) 949-7415.
Fax:	(809) 949-7101.
Courses:	Half day and week long underwater photo classes, PADI, NAUI underwater photo specialty.
Photo Processing:	Quality controlled E-6 daily.
Photo Rental:	All Nikonos system, with free mini-lesson; disposable cameras with underwater housing.
Video Rental:	Wide angle, and auto focus, with free mini-lesson.
Camera Repair:	Full service Nikonos repair, all parts in stock.
Special Comments:	World's largest underwater photo centre and gallery.

CLINT EBANK'S SCUBA CAYMAN

Owner/Manager:	Clint Ebanks.
Address:	P.O. Box 746, Grand Cayman.
Telephone:	(809)-949-3873.
No. of Tanks:	160.
Dive Boats - No:	1.
Length & Capacity:	46 ft (25 divers).
Daily Trips:	2 tank morning dive; 1 tank afternoon dive.
Night Dives:	On request.
Special Dives:	On request.

PIRATE'S POINT RESORT

Owner/Manager:	Gladys Howard, Larry Smith.
Address:	Little Cayman, Cayman Islands.
Telephone:	(809)-948-4210.
No. of Tanks:	30.
Dive Boats - No:	2.
Length & Capacity:	1x18 ft (6 divers); 1x16 ft (4 divers).
Daily Trips:	2 tank morning dive.
Night Dives:	On request.
Special Dives:	Bloody Bay Wall.
Accommodation:	Beach cottages.
Dive Shop:	On site.

BEACH CLUB DIVERS

Owner/Manager:	William Burgher.
Address:	P.O. Box 903 GT, Grand Cayman.
Telephone:	(809)-949-8100, (1-8008-PREMIER) (1-800-327-877).
No. of Tanks:	84.
Dive Boats - No:	2.
Length & Capacity:	1x38 ft V-hull (20 divers); 1x34 ft (16 divers).
Daily Trips:	2 tank morning dive;
Night Dives:	On request.
Special Dives:	Stingray City, others on request.
Resort Courses:	Daily.
Courses:	Certification courses to all levels.
Photo Processing:	No..
Photo Rental:	Yes.
Video Rental:	Yes.
Accommodation:	41 air-conditioned rooms.
Dive Shop:	On site.

SPANISH BAY REEF ALL INCLUSIVE RESORT

Owner/Manager:	Mark Mclaughin.
Address:	P.O. Box 903 GT, Grand Cayman.
Telephone:	(809)-949-3765, (1-8008-PREMIER) (1-800-327-877).
No. of Tanks:	94.
Dive Boats - No:	2.
Length & Capacity:	1x38 ft V-hull (20 divers); 1x34 ft (16 divers).
Daily Trips:	2 tank morning dive;
Unlimited:	Shore diving.
Night Dives:	On request.
Special Dives:	On request.
Resort Courses:	Daily.
Courses:	Certification courses to all levels.
Photo Processing:	No.
Photo Rental:	Yes.
Video Rental:	No.
Accommodation:	50 air-conditioned rooms.
Dive Shop:	On site.

CAYMAN DIVING LODGE

Owner/Manager:	Bob Autry, Butch Belanger, Kathy Belanger
Address:	P.O. Box 11, East End, Grand Cayman.
Telephone:	(809)-947-7555,
No. of Tanks:	60
Dive Boats - No:	3.
Length & Capacity:	1x42 ft (20 divers); 1x32 ft (12 divers); 1x32 ft (12 divers).
Daily Trips:	2 tank morning dives; 1 tank afternoon dive; unlimited shore diving.
Night Dives:	On request.
Accommodation:	16 sea front units.

PETER MILBURN'S DIVE CAYMAN LTD.

Owner/Manager:	Peter Milburn.
Address:	P.O. Box 59 6 Grand Cayman.
Telephone:	(809)-947-4341.
Fax:	(809)-947-2524.
No. of Tanks:	120.
Dive Boats - No:	3.
Length & Capacity:	1x28 ft (10 divers); 1x32 ft (12 divers); 1x36 ft (16 divers).
Daily Trips:	2 tank morning dive; 1 tank afternoon dive.
Night Dives:	On request.
Special Dives:	Yes.

SURFSIDE WATERSPORTS.

Owner/Manager:	Bob Carter.
Address:	P.O. Box 891, George Town, Grand Cayman.
Telephone:	(809) 949-7330.
Fax:	(809) 949-8639.
No. of Tanks:	180.
Dive Boats - No.:	4.
Length & Capacity:	1x38 ft (20 divers); 1x36 ft (15 divers); 1x40 ft (20 divers); 1x40 ft (25 divers).
Daily Trips:	2 Tank morning dives; 1 tank afternoon dives & snorkel trips.
Night Dives:	Yes.
Special Dives:	Stingray trips 5 times weekly from Rum Point.
Resort Courses:	Daily.
Courses:	Certification & more than 20 specialties.
Photo Processing:	No.
Photo Rental:	35mm Sea & Sea, Nikonos.
Video Rental:	Personal and group video shot by SURFSIDE.
Accommodation:	Packages available with 6 location options. A hotel, 4 different condominiums and cottages offered.
Dive Shop:	2 Shops, located in George Town and Rum Point (809) 947-9098.

FISHING AND WATERSPORTS

C & G WATERSPORTS

Owner/Manager	Crosby Ebanks
Address:	P.O. Box 714, George Town, Grand Cayman.
Telephone:	(809)-947-4049.
Snorkel/ Fishing Boats:	3.
Length & Capacity:	47ft Trimaran (50 passengers); 40ft Trimaran (35 passengers); 36ft Power boat (20 passengers).
Daily Trips:	5 hr Snorkel trip on sailboat including conch diving, reef snorkeling, Stingray City, hot seafood lunch. 3.5 hr Light tackle fishing (bottom/reef, bonefish, tarpon). Bait, tackle and soft drinks provided.
Shop:	Retail store — C & G WATERSPORTS, Coconut Place, West Bay Road.

EDEN ROCK

Owner/Manager:	Stuart Freeman.
Address:	P.O. Box 1907, South Church Street, George Town, Grand Cayman.
Telephone:	(809) 949-7243.
Fax:	(809) 949-0842.
No. of Tanks:	120.
Dive Boats - No:	1.
Length & Capacity:	1x25 ft (8 divers).
Daily Trips:	Small group 2 and 1 tank dive available.
Night Dives:	Shore night dives nightly, to Eden Rocks and Devil's Grotto.
Special Dives:	Including a get back into diving program.
Resort Courses:	Resort courses and repeat resorts (one of our specialty's) taught at 8am. 10am. 12pm. 1.30pm. and 3.30pm. daily dives on Eden Rocks or Devils Grotto.
Courses:	Student referrals, Full certification to Asst. instructor. NAUI pro center, PADI International facility, and BSAC school.
Photo Processing:	No.
Photo Rental:	Yes.
Video Rental:	No.
Accommodation:	No.
Dive Shop:	Retail, rental, fills, hydro and repairs located on South Church Street a few minutes walk from George Town Harbor.
Special Comments:	Eden Rock Diving Center offers a unique opportunity for both divers and snorkeler to enjoy two of Caymans best shallow water reefs for as little as the rental of their equipment, easy shore access to Eden Rock and Devil's Grotto.

RIVERS SPORT DIVERS LTD.

Owner/Manager:	Wallace Lynn Rivers.
Address:	West Bay, P.O. Box 442, Grand Cayman.
Telephone:	(809)-949-1181.
No. of Tanks:	75.
Dive Boats - No:	1.
Length & Capacity:	34 ft (14 Divers).
Daily Trips:	2 tank morning dive, 1 tank afternoon dive, night dives.
Special Dives:	Stingray City.
Resort Courses:	PADI, NAUI certification.
Dive Shop:	In West Bay.

SUBMARINE DIVES

RESEARCH SUBMERSIBLES LTD.

Owner/Manager	Robyn Woodward.
Address:	P.O. Box 1719, Grand Cayman.
Telephone:	(809)-949-8296.
Fax:	(809)-949-7421.
Submarines:	2, capacity of 2 passengers per sub.
Daily Trips:	4 - 5 dives, Monday through Saturday at 9am. 10:30am. 12pm. 1:30pm. 3pm.
Shop:	Located on North Church Street, George Town, next door to the drive-in window side of Burger King on the waterfront.

FURTHER READING

Williams, N., *A History of the Cayman Islands,* Government of the Cayman Islands, 1970.

Pitcairn, F. and Humann, P., *Cayman Underwater Paradise,* Reef Dwellers Press, Bryn Athyn, 1979.

Sefton, N., *Dive Cayman,* Undersea Photo Supply of Cayman, 1981.

Roessler, C., *Diving Snorkeling Guide to Grand Cayman,* Pisces Books, 1984.

SEAPEN'S DIVER'S GUIDES

The ultimate tools for dive tourists to these areas. Landmarks, dive sites, depths, approaches and other essential facts are brought to life using aerial photographs, 3-D techniques and stunning graphics. Transparent overlays and schematic drawings help the diver orient himself both above and below the waterline. Tips on underwater photography methods, a Fish Index listing the most commonly-sighted species and Dive Service Guidelines make each guide an essential and popular diving accessory.

The Diver's Guide Series includes complete information on dive sites in:

RED SEA DIVER'S GUIDE: Eilat to Ras Muhammed, available in English, German and French editions.

BAHAMAS DIVER'S GUIDE: Grand Bahama in the north to Exuma Island in the south.

CAYMAN DIVER'S GUIDE: Grand Cayman, Little Cayman and Cayman Brac.

FLORIDA KEYS DIVER'S GUIDE: The Upper Keys, Key Largo and Islamorada.

Each volume in the DIVER'S GUIDE series measures 27x15cm and is printed in full color on 120g chrome paper with a laminated soft cover.

Look for other quality **SEAPEN** marine publications:

SHARKS OF THE RED SEA: A stunning rendition of the varieties found in the Red Sea, drawn from the diver's perspective with a concise description of each shark.

RAYS OF THE CARIBBEAN: Portrays the Caribbean rays clearly and definitively.

FISHTRICKS: Introduces 132 sea creatures previously unknown to man – 'discovered' by Shlomo Cohen .

CALLIGRAFISH: New, cleverly adapted sea creatures. These amusing glimpses of marine life make unbeatable promotional gifts.

SEAPEN T-SHIRTS: A wide range of marine prints, from the completely realistic to the slightly amazing. These must simply be seen to be believed. High quality silk screening on 100% cotton.

IF YOU'VE ENJOYED OUR MARINE PUBLICATIONS, LOOK FOR OUR OTHER PUBLICATIONS:
Sex A to Z, Bible A to Z, Columbus Log A to Z, which appear as calendars, posters and diaries.